SEEDS OF CHANGE

SEEDS OF CHANGE

The spiritual quest of Kerry Livgren

Revised and Expanded Edition

by Kerry Livgren and Kenneth Boa

SPARROW PRESS
Nashville, USA

Library of Congress Catalogue Card Number   91 - 0600 72

ISBN 0-91714-303-5 (Word(UK) edition 0-85009-248-5)

The publisher would like to express appreciation for permission to quote lyrics from the following songs:

Copyright © by Maclen Music, Inc.: "Tomorrow Never Knows."

Copyright © by Don Kirshner Music, Inc.: (1973) "Belexes "; (1974) "Journey from Mariabronn," "Apercu"; (1975) "Incomudro," "Lamplight Symphony," "Two Cents Worth," "Child of Innocence," "Mysteries and Mayhem," "The Pinnacle"; (1976) "Carry on Wayward Son," "The Wall," "Miracles Out of Nowhere," "Opus Insert," "Cheyenne Anthem"; (1977) "Dust in the Wind," "Paradox," "Sparks of the Tempest," "Hopelessly Human."

Copyright © Don Kirshner Music, Inc./Blackwood Music Publishing : (1979) "On the Other Side," "A Glimpse of Home"; (1980) "Just One Way," "Mask of the Great Deceiver," "Ground Zero," "Relentless," :No One Together"; (1982) "Fair Exchange," "Diamonds and Pearls," "Windows," "Borderline," "Crossfire."

Copyright © Don Kirshner Music, Inc./Blackwood Music Publishing, Full Grown Music and Mastodon Music: (1982) "Play On."

Cover and Interior design: Jeff Barnes.

Reproduced, printed and bound in the U.K. by Richard Clay Ltd. Bungay.

This book is lovingly dedicated to our wives,
Victoria Livgren
and
Karen Boa

CONTENTS

Preface

PART I

PART II (1990)

With Victoria, Kyle and Katy

Outdoors on "Crossfire Farm"

In "The Peach" Recording Studio

Toto, I Don't Think We're in Kansas Anymore

SEEDS OF CHANGE

PREFACE

This is not another "celebrity biography." The value of a person's thoughts and actions is not dependent on the number of people who know him. Kerry's story is important in itself, not because of his fame.

I met Kerry in the summer of 1979, about a month after he came to the resolution of his spiritual quest. As we got to know each other, it became obvious that we had traveled down similar paths over the years, and it was fascinating to discover the process that gradually led us both to the same conclusions.

When we agreed to work together on this project in 1981, I wondered whether it would be more appropriate to use the first or the third person throughout the book. As I reflected on the many parallels in our lives, I decided to use the first person. In this way, *Seeds of Change* became a synthesis of our minds because I had to insert my thoughts and imagination into his experiences and thought processes. We hope that the product will enable you to think more clearly about your own spiritual journey.

Kenneth Boa
Atlanta, Georgia

REFLECTIONS

A backup rock band often finds itself precariously hovering between the twin extremes of rejection and acceptance. The members of the group know only too well that the audience did not pay to see them—they're simply not the "main event." From beginning to end, they must struggle to convince the audience that though they may not be well-known, they are not second-rate. If they have any ambition, any hopes of future recognition, every song will plead, "We're not just prepping you for the big act to follow—we stand on our own musical ground!"

As I stood offstage and watched our backup group make that musical statement at the close of their act, I suddenly found myself gazing upon my own face and those of the other members of the Kansas band only a few years ago. We were in the same unstable position as those musicians before me, and in that moment of identification the audience's receptive applause filled me with joy. Their success rekindled the memory of our own dreams during those uncertain years.

The audience got more than it expected.

The lights went on, and all through the din of thousands of conversations the roadies scrambled to take down one set of equipment and get our own in place. Preparations for our show had begun early that morning, and the truckloads of paraphernalia including backdrops, amplification equipment, lights, speakers, and instruments were all checked and ready to go. As the lights in the colosseum began to fade, 20,000 voices combined in a roar that filled the place with the electricity of anticipation.

Hundreds of cigarette lighters and matches pierced the darkness, and the chaos of applause was transmuted into a regular cadence of clapping and foot-stamping as the audience rhythmically chanted, "Kansas! Kansas!"

The audience began to hear music, but it certainly wasn't what they expected—they found themselves listening to a recording of the Prelude to Act III of Richard Wagner's *Lohengrin*! For many, this is an unorthodox way to begin a rock concert, but Wagner's majestic theme created a mood of exhilaration that readied the audience for what was to follow. In the darkness the six of us walked on stage, picked up our instruments, and blended in with the recorded music so that when the lights suddenly came on, the audience found us already playing our own version of what they had just been hearing. To add to the effect, smoke was rising from the stage and a green laser light began to create images of musical instruments that hovered and rotated above us with the illusion of three dimensions. When the laser spelled out the word *Kansas* and made it turn about and rotate as a unit, the audience responded with wild enthusiasm. The show had begun.

As we played songs that night from *Audiovisions* and earlier albums, I found myself participating in the music, but my mind was conjuring up images from the past. Retracing my own intellectual and spiritual pilgrimage during the course of my life, I was amazed at the diversity of beliefs I had embraced and rejected. A relentless pursuit of meaning had driven me down a variety of Western and Eastern paths; some led farther than others, and yet all seemed to terminate in dead ends. But what I found in 1979 was not another end but the beginning of a new quality of life that gets richer with every passing month. . . .

CHRISTIAN ROOTS

Topeka, Kansas, September 18, 1949—Allen and Betty Livgren, both working for the Santa Fe Railroad, had their first child. We lived in a tiny one-room house which was in back of another house, and it was there that my father's jazz band practiced for weekend appearances at small clubs.

It's interesting that my first memory is associated with music. I actually remember standing up in my crib, and when the music started to play I bounced up and down in the crib to their music. Memory is strangely selective; my mind draws a complete blank from that time until I was about five years old. It was then that my father and grandfather built a house out in a rural area of Topeka. It was still a modest house, but vastly superior to the first; at least it had more than one room!

The impact of parents upon a person's self-image and later way of life can hardly be overestimated. I look with gratitude upon my father and mother because of their consistent love and integrity. My father was a stern disciplinarian, but he never took it too far. To this day I see him as one of the most honest and straightforward men I have ever met, and (this is probably too rare) I continue to look up to him. His firm sense of principle was always seasoned by kindness and love, and he knew how to spend quality time with his children. He'd hug us, hold us, tell us stories, and take us fishing and hunting—he was great!

My mother was responsible for filling our home with laughter. Her sense of humor and wonderful cooking enriched my life; even now my appreciation for well-prepared food knows few bounds.

When it came to movies, my mother was a real character. She grew up in Kansas City, and her family lived above a movie theater. For years, she saw every movie that played in that theater by simply going downstairs. As a result, she turned into a movie buff who seemed to know everything about the films we watched together on TV.

Both of my parents gave me a desire to be like them. I emulated their goodness and righteousness as well as their kindness and love. At this point in my life, this was something that affected me more than anything I learned at church or school. This mutual love and respect molded me, but as is so often the case, I have only recently come to appreciate what they did for me.

I always loved my parents, and our disagreements were few in spite of the fact that I was a typical brat on many occasions that I can only too readily recall. Naturally, when my younger brothers and sister came along I still wanted to be the center of attention. The four of us weren't maliciously bad, but we caused our parents a lot of grief. Our crazy games became notorious, and our imaginations were rampant. We spent several summers with our cousins in rural Missouri. Those times on the farm were important to me because they instilled a real appreciation for the beauty and complexity of nature in my young mind.

It would be difficult for me to imagine a more wholesome environment than what I encountered as a child, but I sometimes did things that "distorted" that environment. When I was about five, I joined forces with my friend across the street, and together we decided to help out with the construction of one of the houses that was going up in our neighborhood. A new neighbor was getting ready to pour his driveway, so the two of us ambled up to his garage. No one was home, but there was a big cement mixer and several bags of cement in the garage. We decided to surprise him by tearing open those bags of cement, dumping them everywhere, and turning the hose on the whole mess. The owner was surprised all right, but for some reason he wasn't thrilled with the masses of concrete that awaited him.

A less "innocent" childhood venture began when I decided to play mailman with a little retarded boy I met. We pulled my red wagon along the road and filled it with mail from practically every mailbox in the neighborhood. We had mounds of mail—people's paychecks, letters and magazines. Our labors done, we carted it all back to the "post office" (my house). There we opened up about half of it and began to throw the rest away. I grew tired of "processing" the mail, but the other boy wanted to take it with him so he could continue playing mailman. So we threw it all in a sack and he took it home. That evening, during dinner, there was a knock at the door. I heard my father talking in low tones with someone at the door. Suddenly he said, "Kerry, get in here!" I knew I was in trouble, but I didn't know why. When I got to the door, I saw three FBI men who were very concerned about someone tampering with the U. S. mail. I categorically denied having anything to do with it, although I was scared out of my wits. But I did happen to mention that I had witnessed a little retarded boy going around taking mail out of everyone's mailbox. The poor kid was too "out of it" to be able to implicate me, so I knew I had gotten off the hook. But that really bothered me; my conscience ate away at me for doing that.

Perhaps it was retribution, but that Halloween my mother made a strange-looking Chinese costume for me to wear, and she completed the effect by putting a stocking over my head to distort my features. I went out to trick-or-treat, but in the darkness I fell into a sewer trench, and the concrete pipe I hit knocked the wind out of me. Some adult came over to inspect the source of the groans he heard, and when his flashlight illuminated a writhing creature with a grotesque face and exotic clothing, his immediate response was, "What th' haell's that??" This did a lot for my self-image!

I remember going to a couple of different churches before my parents finally decided to become members of the Trinity Lutheran Church in Topeka. At that time, this church was part of the Augustana Synod, which was in effect the Swedish branch of the Lutheran Church in America. My father evidently settled on this because he was of Swedish extraction. Apart from Sunday mornings at church, the extent of our Christian involvement was some talk of God and prayers at mealtime.

When I was in church I had little interest in what was going on in the service; my thoughts usually turned to the afternoon when I would be "released" to play with my friends. But there were two things about church that sometimes captivated my mind: the organ music and the stained-glass window above the altar. The music filled me with a sense of reverence and mystery, and while listening to it I would stare at the pastoral scene portrayed in the colored light beaming through the window. It was a picture of Christ shepherding a flock of sheep in a valley. I did not know how to direct these fleeting feelings of mystery and awe, but the sense of longing they produced became an important theme in my later life.

I enjoyed the church services more after I became one of the acolytes. We would put on our white robes, come out the side door next to the altar at the beginning of the service, ceremonially light the candles, and sit on a side bench close to the organ. When the service was over, we put out the candles one by one—there were three on each side of the altar, and I assumed they represented the Trinity. I felt privileged to have an active part in the liturgy.

It was not only the music I heard in church that gave me a sense of reverence and longing. The same thing happened to me in school when my fourth grade teacher played records for us in class. She was especially fond of Tchaikovsky's *1812 Overture,* and every time I heard it I closed my eyes and let my imagination run wild from beginning to end. I knew the music was supposed to portray a specific battle and a victory, but to me it depicted more than an earthly conflict. It came to symbolize the *idea* of conflict and resolution, and this concept remained with me and profoundly influenced my later musical life and overall philosophy. Titanic conflict and triumphant consummation became motifs that frequently surfaced in my spiritual journey in the years to come.

But the person who really exposed me to the world of classical music was my Aunt Lily. This intelligent and perceptive woman came to fill the gap that was suddenly opened when both of my grandmothers died in the same week. To have both of them snatched out of earthly existence so quickly was overwhelming and very sobering. I was close to my grandmothers, and this confrontation with the starkness and finality of death filled me with fear. The memory of two funerals with open caskets, flowers and weeping haunted me. This was a kind of turning point in my life; I became less frivolous and more serious in my thinking, even at the tender age of nine.

I began to spend more time at Aunt Lily's house and grew to have a great appreciation for her. She often took me upstairs to hear old classical recordings on her record player. We sat together, listened to the music, and talked about it when it was over. I began to get into the music of Handel, Mendelssohn and Franck because it triggered my imagination in the same way the *1812 Overture* had done before. The majestic images of beauty, power and grandeur that it evoked for me were absent in the music of my peer group, for whom Elvis Presley reigned supreme. Although I would later get very involved with contemporary music, at the time I thought the kids at school were crazy because of their taste; it turned out that they thought the same of me.

During these years, my thinking was also shaped by a number of movies. My family drove to Kansas City to see *Ben Hur*, and for four hours I was completely lost in the film. I was stunned; when it was over I didn't want to come out. This film, along with other big production films loosely based on the Bible, like *The Ten Commandments* and *King of Kings*, did more to bring home the idea of God in Christ than anything I had read in the Bible, because of the musical scores and lavish imagery. But at that time I hardly understood a thing about the Bible.

When I went into the sixth grade, I was able to see more movies than ever. I became a junior safety patrolman, and we were rewarded for our patrol work with passes to movies. Every weekend I watched a double feature at one theater, and then walked over to another theater to see one or two more. It's a wonder that I didn't develop chronic conjunctivitis! Besides films like *Ben Hur* and *The Ten Commandments*, I was also impressed by movies that used special effects to create fantasy worlds, like

The Seventh Voyage of Sinbad and *Journey to the Center of the Earth.*
In the same way, I loved books that fired my imagination, such
as those on Greek mythology and Celtic history. Music, movies
and books combined to stimulate my already active imagination, and while this was beneficial in some ways it didn't exactly
help me in school. I had a burning desire to learn, but my
problem was that the subjects I wanted to learn about didn't
correspond well with the things I was supposed to learn in
school. I was more proficient at daydreaming than at classwork.

Because I was such an oddball, I established a social position in grade school which was to stay with me all the way
through high school and college. I was an unpopular kid, having
little association with my peers, few friends, and never being a
member of an "in" crowd. I was torn in two directions; part of
me resented it, but another part was actually proud that I was
not involved with a clique. I wanted very much to be accepted
and to be a part of things in school, but at the same time I
developed a fierce independence because of a feeling that something would be taken away from me if I achieved social approv-
al. Because of this inner warfare, I consciously strove to develop
different interests. Everyone else seemed to be involved in sports,
so I decided to listen to classical music and build model air-
planes. I wanted to be set apart, but this was the very thing that
caused me pain. I remember many times coming home to my
mother and saying, "Mom, nobody likes me; I'm not accepted."

This was obvious even on my first day as a junior patrolman. I was so proud of my new belt, and I was given the
desirable assignment of standing by Shunganunga Creek. Just
as I was thinking of what a great day it was, along came a group
of punks. They picked me up, threw me into the creek, and
continued walking to school. I was crushed; an era had ended.

To summarize my world view at the time, my parents had
implanted in me a longing for righteousness and goodness. The
strong moral consciousness they imparted affected the rest of
my life. The excellent environment in which I was raised also
gave me the freedom to develop my imagination. Early exposure to music, films and books produced a longing in me for
beauty and meaning. During these years, I was a nominal Chris-

tian; but apart from my limited involvement in church, I understood little of what Christianity meant.

The death of my grandmothers and later the Cuban missile
crisis and assassination of John F. Kennedy taught me that life
on this planet is unstable—everything can pass away in a moment. I realized that tragedy was a real possibility and that
nothing around me was permanent.

2

THE QUEST BEGINS

I was confirmed at Trinity Lutheran Church at the age of thirteen after going through the required process of learning and memorization. I came to respect and admire Pastor Nelson, and though my mind often wandered in confirmation class he managed to communicate the concepts we needed to learn. We studied the cardinal doctrines of Christianity and elements of church history. We were also required to recite the Apostles' Creed, the Nicene Creed, and the answers to catechismal questions.

My interest in spiritual matters was minimal; so the spiritual answers I was learning didn't correspond to the questions I was raising. Thus, I understood the material on an intellectual level, but I was unable to grasp what it really meant; I had "ears to hear," but I didn't hear. It amazes me now to look back on this period of time and recall the explicit details I was given concerning the person and work of Christ, and yet how little it mattered to me. I suspect the same was true of most of the other members of that class. If someone had asked me at that time what it really meant to be a Christian, my answer would have been an abysmal fabric of confusion.

Upon entering junior high school, I experienced another kind of confirmation. I finally succumbed to the powerful pull of peer pressure. My earlier exposure to jazz (my father's jazz band), classical music (Aunt Lily), and film scores gave me musical tastes which did not fit those of my age group. Now I found that my interests had broadened to include popular music and girls. I had become a full-fledged adolescent.

The most significant thing that happened to me during this time was my discovery of a kindred spirit in the person of Timothy Scott Strauss. It was almost as though someone had planned our friendship; for a period of two years our class schedules were absolutely identical. Regardless of what subjects I chose or what sections I was placed in, there he was in every one of my classes. As we got to know each other, we discovered that there was also an uncanny similarity in our backgrounds and interests. We were both Lutherans, though his church was part of the Missouri Synod while mine was in the Augustana Synod. Both of us were interested in the same films, the same books, and especially the same music. Nevertheless, I often felt that I was standing in his shadow because of the keenness of his mind. His brilliance was not directed at achieving straight A's in school but at wrestling with advanced concepts. Tim was also blessed with striking features; he was handsome and strong.

Our mutual interest in music became our strongest bond. Neither of us played an instrument, but Tim was responsible for our decision to begin. We used to go to a recreation center for junior high students to see rock 'n' roll bands play. We were absolutely floored by the power of the music. It was so much fun and such a relief from the awkwardness and pressure of being adolescents that we decided to join in.

Up until that time my only experience with an instrument consisted of a few piano lessons; my keyboard skill was rudimentary, if even that. We both knew that guitars were our calling in the world of rock 'n' roll; nothing else was "cool" at the time, so we simply had to learn.

My first electric guitar was one I made myself out of a Stella, one of the cheapest guitars made. I took an old Sears amplifier that my Dad had and a low quality astatic microphone and taped the microphone to the inside of the guitar. When I plugged it into the amplifier, my electric guitar was complete. Unfortunately, I couldn't turn it above conversational level because it would feed back. But it whetted my appetite for bigger and better things in musical instruments.

I was immediately jealous of Tim, who went out to Sears and bought a real electric guitar. So I began to apply pressure to my parents. My Dad finally relented and took me to my Uncle Ole's music store in Topeka. There he bought me a Kay electric guitar. My musical career had begun.

This balanced our relationship. While Tim always seemed to be one step ahead of me intellectually, I was always the one who taught him how to play and what to play. I was the lead guitarist, and Tim played rhythm guitar. At the time we absolutely idolized a group called The Ventures. This was right at the peak of the surf music period. As I look back on it, this kind of music seems so corny, but at that time the idea of surfers, freedom and sunshine was very attractive to us. Our favorite Ventures song was called "Pipeline," and it became one of the first songs we learned.

I think the quality that drew me to The Ventures was their distinctive musical style. They didn't write all of the music they played, but they had an element of originality that set them apart from most other groups in that period. It was this *originality* that I found myself emulating. Thus, our method of imitating The Ventures was not to reproduce their sound but to create our own distinctive sound. This became our point of departure from most of the other young musicians we knew. They wanted to be very much like the popular artists in the way they *played* their music; we wanted to be like them in the way they *wrote* their music. And the best popular groups were those whose originality set them apart from others.

There were many other things that bound Tim and me together. One of these was a nonsense philosophy we developed and called "Liropi." This was a light-hearted world view based upon the approach to life found in the Marx Brothers films and the Bob Hope/Bing Crosby "Road"pictures. For awhile, we tried to live in the fantasy world of Liropi as if we were in one of the Road pictures ourselves. Hence the name Liropi—Living Road Picture. An even sillier invention was The Cheerful Canary Club. This club met in the restrooms after school to read absurd poems and tell awful jokes. The entire roster of the club consisted of the two of us. (One of our Cheerful Canary meetings was broken up when some tough guys walked in the restroom and threw my math book in the towel disposal unit. When they left, I tried to retrieve it by reaching in, but my head got stuck. The metal flap allowed me to put my head in but not to take it out. I thought it would take forever for Tim to get the janitor.)

In spite of our adolescent lunacy, Tim and I began to make more serious and thoughtful discoveries. These included the music of Richard Wagner and Richard Strauss and the philosophy of Friedrich Nietzsche. In these areas, Tim was the innovator and I was the follower. These things were above my head, and he forced me to stretch higher to reach them. I began to find to my own pleasure that I had a capacity to enter into this world of art, music and philosophy, but it was Tim who always had to lead the way. I was fascinated when he told me about Nietzsche's concept of the *Übermensch* or superman, the man who understands the anguish of the human condition but who triumphs over weakness by establishing his own values and realizing his true potential. The grandiose and sumptuous music of Wagner seemed to fit in well with these concepts, and we used to sit around the stereo for hours at a time listening to *Tannhäuser, Tristan und Isolde,* and my favorite, *Parsifal.* These magnificent music dramas with their interwoven leitmotifs or musical themes frequently overwhelmed us with their power. We sometimes found ourselves transported into a romantic world of mystical and sensory ecstasy.

The symphonic poems of Richard Strauss (Tim Strauss claimed to be distantly related) also influenced us strongly. His *Also sprach Zarathustra (Thus Spoke Zarathustra)* was a musical portrayal of the philosophy of Nietzsche, the title taken from Nietzsche's chief work. This music was later used most effectively by Stanley Kubrick in *2001: A Space Odyssey.* We also loved to listen to *Tod und Verklärung (Death and Transfiguration).* Strauss' effective use of dissonance and resolution in his music brought back that feeling of titanic conflict and triumphant consummation I first had years before when listening to Tchaikovsky's *1812 Overture.*

Needless to say, the philosophy of Nietzsche doesn't exactly blend in with Christianity. So it was strange that at the same time we were exploring all these things, Tim was also getting heavily involved with his church youth group. The pastor appre-

ciated his challenging questions, and his insights made him the
star of the group. But for me, Tim's talk about Nietzsche and
Wagner was far more interesting than learning about Jesus. It
was not long before Tim also began to feel the tension of
hanging on to two radically different approaches to reality.
While we didn't consciously apostasize, we found ourselves gently
drifting away from the moorings of our Christian upbringing.

Neither of us did well in high school, not because we were
incapable, but because we regarded the curriculum as dull and
irrelevant in comparison to our music and our new areas of
discovery. Our little community expanded to include a third
member, an artist named Karl Geiss. Tim and Karl began to
discuss the books of Ayn Rand, including *Atlas Shrugged* and *For
the New Intellectual*. Her philosophy shares several things in common with that of Nietzsche. It is a romanticism that seeks to
elevate man as a heroic being and do away with any sense of
subordination to the mind of another, particualarly God. Her
philosophy of objectivism promotes reason as opposed to "faith"
and "creative selfishness" as opposed to altruism. I had an
interest in these things, but my real area of input in this peer
group was that of music.

For awhile, an unlikely fourth person was added to our
group—my mother! She began to hang out with us as one of
the "guys." All four of us went to a meeting of people who were
involved in Ayn Rand's philosophy, and we all discussed the
concepts afterward. But my mother was most excited about the
band we had started, probably because I was the one who
headed it and wrote all the music.

Popular English groups like The Yardbirds and The Kinks
had a strong influence on my music at that time, but the musical
and philosophical romanticism of Wagner, Strauss, Nietzsche
and Rand profoundly affected not only my music, but my developing world view as well.

We decided to call our band The Gimlets. We wanted
everything about the band to be original, including the name;
so Tim invented the word "gimlet." Or so he thought—we later
found out that someone else had invented it first. A gimlet is a
small tool with a cross handle and a point like a screw that is

used for boring holes. It is also the name of a mixed drink. After this, we learned to check the dictionary before pronouncing a word "original"—it saves a lot of embarrassment! Nevertheless, we decided to stick with the name, or rather we realized that we were already stuck with it.

Another "founding father" of The Gimlets was a good friend I had known since junior high school days named Scott Kessler. Scott and I had a lot in common, including motorcycles, games and so forth; so I wanted to include him in the band as well. In those days you didn't look for musicians; you just found people you liked and hoped they could learn how to play. I helped teach Scott how to play a bass guitar and fortunately he picked it up nicely.

Later when organs came into vogue, we decided that The Gimlets had to have one. We thought of Dan Wright, a friend of ours who had a boisterous, humorous personality, and agreed that he would fit well with the band. We talked his parents into buying him a cheap little organ, and I taught him how to play. This was easy to do, because in that period the worst you had to worry about were songs like "Louie, Louie" and "Wipe Out."

Dan's musical career was marked from the beginning by a streak of bad luck. On his very first gig, his organ tumbled off the stage and fell onto the floor, an embarrassing moment but somehow the organ kept working.

Our original drummer, John Pribble, was the son of a man who worked with my father at Goodyear. We eventually had to let John go because he contracted mononucleosis. We would have lost too many engagements by keeping him on; so we replaced John with Carl Corona. Because Carl was short, he decided to play the drums while standing up, which was something of a novelty.

At first, we stayed in business primarily by playing for the military. We were booked consistently at the Forbes Air Force Base officers' and enlisted mens' clubs, and we played in military service clubs around Kansas. For some reason, these people found us particularly interesting.

During these years, being in a band was very much in vogue. There were so many rock 'n'roll bands and rhythm and blues bands in high school that it became ridiculous. It seemed that everyone, musical talent or not, had to belong to a band. But out of the thirty-five or so bands comprised of students from Topeka West High School, The Gimlets were somewhat unique. We were about the only ones who wrote original songs and music. Almost from the beginning, when we first learned to play our guitars in my garage, I felt an urge to combine my interests in poetry and in music by creating songs for our band. This made us quite unpopular in the eyes of the other students, who thought we were weird. Our originality wasn't appreciated, and people looked down on us for not playing the popular music of the day. We were sometimes discouraged at being labeled "strange" and "screwy"; we preferred to think of ourselves as innovative and progressive. Most of the people who were attracted to our unpopular band were themselves unpopular—an example, I suppose, of "Misery loves company."

Concluding that "A prophet is not without honor except in his home town," we decided to look elsewhere for more fertile ground. We began to set up small weekend engagements all over Kansas and Missouri. It was so easy then—all we needed was a car and a trailer for our equipment, and we were on the road. Twice we went to St. Joseph, Missouri to perform on a local television show called *Let's Dance*. We thought this was our big break and that we had the world by the tail.

As time went on, I became so enthralled with writing and playing music that it adversely affected my education. School-work was less fulfilling to me, and I rationalized that I was learning more by traveling and performing with the band on weekends than I was during the week at school. Playing at clubs, bars and high school dances did, in fact, give me quite an education about human nature. We even played in some strip-tease places before we were old enough to buy beer. As I watched the people from the stage while we performed, the whole bar scene became increasingly unattractive to me. From that point on, I never felt an urge to participate in that kind of environment. In fact, throughout my high school years I was a complete teetotaler. In this area I was even different from the other members of The Gimlets. Like their peers, they periodically got loaded in parks and cars on the weekends. But this never appealed to me. I felt overexposed to drinking just by playing in the bars and honky-tonks. My observations of drunkenness convinced me that I didn't want to experiment with my consciousness in that way. The same thing happened to me when I was later exposed to the growing drug culture. I was generally more interested in observing than in indulging. I was fascinated by people's reactions to these things, but my own participation was limited.

When I graduated from high school in 1967, I devoted more time to music. We had lost our drummer with The Gimlets, and he was replaced by a drummer from Lawrence, Kansas. At that time, Lawrence was the center of the sixties hippie culture in Kansas (because of the University of Kansas). All the intellectuals seemed to hang out in Lawrence, whether they went to the university or not.

Our new drummer introduced the members of the band to marijuana, and I found myself simultaneously repulsed and attracted. By this time, I was already intrigued with the music of the San Francisco groups and with the paraphernalia and philosphies of the counterculture. I thought of it as an exciting movement of "flower power," love and hope, but I didn't want to view it as a drug culture. I was absorbed with what drugs were doing to people's thinking, and I loved to be around people who were on drugs and listen to them talk about their hallucinations and mental patterns. But something within me said "No" to drugs and kept me from participating at that point. Still, it was a very thrilling time, and I knew that important new things were beginning to happen. The rest of the band began to experiment with psychedelics and the summer of 1967 proved to be most interesting. . . .

The timing seemed perfect—I was out of school; I was free. Exciting things were happening culturally and musically, and everyone sensed something unique in the air. To the members of our generation it seemed that humanity was about to turn over a new leaf and begin a new chapter entitled "Love." We thought we were on the brink of a new consciousness, and no one wanted to miss out. I remember listening to the radio a great deal that summer because so many things were happening that had a very profound effect on my whole outlook. I started letting my hair grow long for the first time and dove right into the counterculture.

I became so enthralled in the psychedelic imagery of this time that I constructed a number of devices to heighten my consciousness. One of these I called the "head box." I built a box and placed several mirrors and all kinds of little paintings inside. The box was also equipped with a variety of flashing lights and strobe lights along with two pairs of tiny speakers on the left and right sides. When I placed this box over my head, it seemed to produce images of other worlds. I interpreted them as equivalent to the hallucinogenic visions produced by drugs. I spent hours with my head in that crazy contraption, laying down and listening to groups like The Grateful Dead and Moby Grape, letting my mind drift into a psychedelic wonderland.

The basement of my parents' house became the territory for my regular haunts; the stereo was there, and I was free to create my own environment. It turned into a kind of giant head box as I set up strobe lights and put my paintings on the walls. When my friends came over, we would sit around as though we were on drugs and listen to the music, deluded into thinking that we were piercing through to higher planes of consciousness. We thought it was very heavy and profound to be carried away by songs like "In-A-Gadda-Da-Vida" by the Iron Butterfly or "Light My Fire" by The Doors, when in actuality we were simply a bunch of silly kids.

Some kids from a Congregational church youth group used to have a kind of cabaret in their basement. Everyone would come to sit by candlelight and have rap sessions or listen to music. Someone told them about all the devices in my base-ment, and a group of them came over to see what it was like. I proudly displayed my creations and put "In-A-Gadda-Da-Vida," the anthem of the day, on the turntable to enhance the effect. But when one of them started to pass a marijuana joint around, I got a painfully tense feeling in the pit of my stomach because this was happening in my parents' house. I didn't partake; I was absolutely terrified that my father was going to come downstairs and find out what was going on. As it was, he had a negative attitude toward my basement paraphernalia because he had no idea what it all meant.

Even though I was practically enthralled with the whole counterculture movement, I frequently felt little twinges of guilt and regret. I had definite feelings that something wasn't right about what was happening, but I couldn't discern what it was.

During these months, I was running into more and more differences with my father. He was upset with my physical appearance, but he was even more concerned about my future. It was obvious in the last couple of years that my greatest interest in life was music. As a jazz musician, my father could understand a love of music; but for him it was only a supplementary form of income on weekends. It wasn't something you did as a full-time vocation. His brother (my Uncle Ole) attempted a successfuel full-time career at playing music. He made a living, but it really wasn't the thing my father had in mind. Parents naturally want their children to be better off than they were, and my father was no exception. He had big dreams for me, but he could see them drifting away from him as I got more interested in music and the counterculture.

To make matters worse, I suddenly found myself faced with the trauma of a major decision. Late in the summer, my father got transferred to the Goodyear plant in Akron, Ohio. I had to decide to go with my family or stay with the band. It was time to leave home and go to college anyway, and I still believed in the band and wanted it to succeed. It was difficult to let my family go, especially because we had always been so close, but I opted to stay with my music and my friends. To stay in Topeka, I enrolled that fall in Washburn University. My parents were at least pleased that I decided to go to college.

Still, I looked upon college with a great deal of reservation because I didn't really know why I was going. I wanted to learn things, but what was happening with my generation appeared to be so much more significant. I was convinced that I could achieve greater enlightenment along that path than in an institution of higher learning. But as long as I could keep developing musically, perhaps I could have the best of both worlds.

The Gimlets were still together, but the nature of the band was changing, partly because of my growing obsession to do more original songs. I desperately wanted to be a part of this period of flowering originality in music. Of course, the more I pursued this passion, the more it hurt our commercial acceptance. Very few groups in our area were doing original music at the time. Our unpopularity led to chronic insolvency throughout the brief history of The Gimlets.

My world view was confused in this period because I was unable to sort out all the new concepts and philosophies that were bombarding me. Certainly by this time I had all but shelved my Christian upbringing. On the one hand, I was no longer interested in the more familiar thought patterns, and on the other I was afraid to consider the implications these new ideas had in relation to Christianity. I knew I had rejected traditional Christianity, but I couldn't bring myself to say it just yet. The world seemed to be pulling me in all directions at once, and I wanted some way of putting it all together.

The humanistic philosophies of Friedrich Nietzsche and Ayn Rand still influenced my thinking, but unlike them I had not yet come to reject the existence of God. I had practically no interest in the Bible, but the wonders of creation (I especially remember a trip with my family to Yellowstone Park in this connection) sometimes made me feel close to God. This became more of a nature mysticism as time went on.

Because of my confusion, I tended to focus my attention on music, because that was the one place where I found solace.

"HIGHER" EDUCATION

When my maternal grandfather passed away, he left me $3,000 for my education. This seemed like an astronomical sum at the time, but it gradually disappeared as I dipped into it to pay for college courses and general survival.

So I decided to get a job—hanging draperies in a Topeka department store. There was something different about the person who was training me, and I couldn't put it together at first. But when the manager of the department warned me not to go over to his house, it became clear that the "something different" was his sexual preference. This first encounter with a homosexual was only one contributing factor to my growing disillusionment with the drapery hanging business. My job was not fulfilling any needs, so after about a month I terminated my employment (actually, we came to a mutual agreement which led to a termination). At this point, I resolved to support my college career exclusively by music.

For awhile, I had even fewer friends than I did in high school. My little peer group at first consisted entirely of The Gimlets, but even here our attitudes were beginning to change. We realized that our music had now become our source of financial support, as opposed to something we did on weekends for a lark in high school.

Before my parents moved away from Kansas, I had become good friends with Don Sligar, the drummer for Morning Dew, another band in Topeka. Don and I decided to find an apartment together, and our search led us to an old and well-worn house near downtown Topeka. Our apartment was on the first floor, and there were other tenants on the two floors above us. It was ironic that directly across the street and within a stone's throw was Trinity Lutheran Church, the church of my childhood years, confirmation and duties as a young acolyte. Every time I looked out my window, the steeple spires would relentlessly remind me of religious beliefs, liturgies and activities that now seemed so foreign to me. The church building had become a shell, stripped of its former mysteries, and I had no desire to visit.

It is very difficult for me to nail down my true motivations for going to college. Certainly the growing pressure of the draft at this time played a role in my thinking, because the war in Vietnam seemed so senseless to me. But there were other reasons. I had a fierce desire to learn, to find answers, to put things together in my thinking. Yet my three years at Washburn University did not quench that raging thirst for knowledge. In fact, I became more and more disillusioned with school as I began to perceive the real nature of what I wanted to learn. Mathematics, history, biology and so forth were interesting, sometimes fascinating, but they never seemed to get to the core of what life was all about. I had a longing for a knowledge that was not compartmentalized, something that would tie all these disciplines together. I wanted answers about human existence, and about my own existence in particular.

The more courses I took, the more confused I became, and my college years turned out to be the bleakest time of my life. I felt a tremendous urge to justify my own existence in some way, to achieve something that would lift this burden off my shoulders. I wanted to know who I was as a person, why I was on this planet, and what I was going to do with my life as a result. My search seemed to be moving in the direction of the nontemporal, but I didn't know where to look for answers, if indeed there were any.

Only one course came close to satisfying some of that urge during my days in college. Not surprisingly, it was a course on world religions. In it, we studied the backgrounds and teachings of each of the major religions of the world. This opened up new realms of thought for me, since each of these religions dealt with the basic questions I was beginning to struggle with at this time: What is ultimate reality? What is the nature and destiny of man? Where is history going?

The last religion we examined was Christianity. Strangely, I found it to be the least compelling and interesting of all the world religions. Perhaps this was because I already knew or thought I knew what Christianity was all about.

At the end of the course, someone asked the professor what he personally believed. He had carefully avoided making any critical judgment of the tenets of the various religions, and we had no idea of his own convictions. To me, he was a fascinating teacher, and having established a rapport with him over the semester I really wanted to know his opinion. I was so disappointed with his answer: "Well, I'm a Christian, and I'm of the Baptist denomination." I had already "tried" Christianity and drifted away from it; the religions of the East seemed so much more profound and alluring. It was a real letdown to find out that this intriguing professor whose opinion I had come to respect turned out to be just another churchgoing Christian, and a Baptist at that! Later I would discover that I hardly had any conception of what Christianity was actually about.

Because of general uncertainty over my vocational interests, I did not exactly excel as a student. I found that my interest level in the subjects I was being taught was often directly proportional to the interest level the instructors had in teaching them, and in most cases this was fairly low. I kept deferring the decision about my major subject until the dean finally called me into his office and said, "Look, you have to declare a major. You must decide what you're going to do, what direction you're going to take." But the only growing commitment I had during this time was in the area of music. The problem was that I could find no practical outlet for my music courses. I had no desire to be a music teacher or a band leader. It began to dawn on me that the kind of thing I really wanted to do with music was not something I could learn about in school. It was something I would have to develop within myself, and to do so would require a total commitment. This would mean a radical change in the direction of my life, and I found the prospect at once exciting and frightening. I could no longer conform to the image my school and my parents had carved out for me, and this resulted in a lot of confusion.

It still amazes me to think that during the entire time I was in high school and college, I never had a single date, let alone a girlfriend. Yet I had a strong interest in the opposite sex and even tended to fall head over heels in love with whatever walked past me. I was always considered heady and off in the clouds, and I never seemed to run into any girls who wanted to discuss the things I was most interested in. Because of this difficulty, the most natural thing was to withdraw and make myself unavailable. This became a vicious circle: the more I withdrew from women, the more self-conscious I became in their presence, and this led in turn to further withdrawal. It was only after college that I was able to break out of this syndrome.

My interest in the whole counterculture movement continued to grow during the three years I spent in college. The psychedelic culture, however, was not well received in a conservative midwestern college like Washburn. There were a few people in the SDS, but I was never involved with the political aspect of what was going on in the late sixties. My infatuation was with what was happening in the drug culture (though not so much with the drugs themselves), especially the music, the imagery, and the apparent hope and optimism. It seemed to be a time of great change and opening up of new ideas, new directions, new dimensions. All of this was strongly resisted by most of the Washburn students in these years. Fraternities still reigned supreme, and hippies were often regarded with scorn. It was not until the early seventies that the counterculture movement begun on the east and west coasts (notably Greenwich Village and Berkeley) would infiltrate small campuses across the country, and ironically by that time the movement was for the most part dead in the places of its origination.

My friends and I were getting bored with the midwestern environment, and we began to do more traveling. On one occasion in the summer of 1969, three of us got into our band van and embarked on a trek to the mountains of Colorado. While we were in Denver, we decided to go to a movie theatre to see Stanley Kubrick's *2001: A Space Odyssey.* It is difficult to communicate what a powerful impression this film left on my thinking. It was not the science fiction part that really got to me; it was the theological implications that I found so disturbing. Kubrick very effectively developed science fiction writer Arthur C. Clarke's concept of the progressive evolution of the human race. Somehow, the concept that the evolution of humanity is being manipulated by some kind of deity or superhuman entity toward a specific end captured my imagination and whetted my hunger for a knowledge of the cosmic destiny of man. According to the scenario in the movie, it was happening in definite predetermined stages, and the "starchild" heading toward earth at the end seemed to represent the next leap in human evolution. Kubrick's use of music in the film was brilliant, and it was no accident that he selected Richard Strauss' *Also sprach Zarathustra (Thus Spoke Zarathustra)* to be the dominant musical theme. This powerful and triumphant music symbolized these upward transformations in man and clearly connected them with Nietzsche's idea of the *Übermensch,* the superman that is about to emerge from man. The combination of concepts, images and music in this film played on my mind and emotions and crystallized my earlier fascination with the philosophy of Nietzsche and the music of Strauss. It filled me with a renewed sense of longing for something beyond man, but I didn't know what it was.

I walked out of the theater stunned, and that feeling frequently invaded me in the months to come. I saw *2001* five more times in the course of the next year, not as much for the film itself as for the thoughts and sensations it evoked in my consciousness.

My growing desire for an encounter with the transcendent began to lead me down the path of mysticism. The whole hippie culture at that time with its drugs, music and undercurrents of Eastern thought became a catalyst in my own spiritual quest. The music that I was writing at this time began to reflect some of these ideas. The lyrics were vague in their allusions to mystical things, and they were not very well written at that point. I was just beginning to explore this new realm, and my footing was uncertain. This was the first time I had dealt with anything other than the typical themes used in most pop songs. Up until this point, most of my songs followed the standard variations on boy-girl relationships.

1969 saw the demise of The Gimlets. The band didn't suddenly disband; it just gradually frittered away. After The Gimlets fell apart, I ended up playing with a predominantly black rhythm and blues group called The Mellotones for about four months. This was a unique and valuable experience, because I was suddenly immersed in a completely different culture musically and socially. But I began to get musically frustrated with what was happening there and wanted to get The Gimlets back together once again.

We re-formed for a short while, but this time we did so without Tim Strauss, the friend who had so profoundly influenced me. We were beginning to experience troubles with the growing threat of military service. Tim decided not to resist, and simply enlisted. Knowing Tim, he probably had more impact on the military than they had on him, but we didn't hear from him again; he disappeared from our lives for several years.

Things were different without Tim, and for this and other reasons it became obvious that The Gimlets just weren't going to last. We had outgrown the earlier philosophy of the band, and I could no longer handle the name.

Don Montre, the keyboard player with The Mellotones, had been the person responsible for getting me into that group. I had known Don in high school, but we were only loosely acquainted at the time. He was playing in a rhythm and blues band, and this was quite different from the kind of pop/English/psychedelic band that I was involved with. But our time together in The Mellotones led to a deep friendship, and we consequently combined our musical resources for several years.

Don left The Mellotones and began to play with a group out in western Kansas called The Reasons Why. This band was a fairly big commercial group, and it was doing quite well financially. I decided to play for The Reasons Why, but the nature of the music and the flashy suits we had to wear annoyed me. Don and I were getting fed up with the whole scene, even though we were making good money. We would sit around and daydream about starting a group and doing original music, something that would be creative, not just commercial.

That drive became so intense that one day we just decided to do it. We dropped out of the group and formed our own band. Two of the old members of The Gimlets—Scott Kessler, the former bass player, and Dan Wright, the former keyboard player—were included in the new band. The rest were new characters, including a lead singer from another town. The small Topeka house I was living in across the street from my old church became the base for the band, and for the first time we plunged into original music.

Our new band was named Saratoga (evidently I got our name off a yellow pencil I was using). I can clearly mark this as the time when I embraced the idea that we were going to make it big in the music business. We seriously began to write and play original music with the goal of becoming a popular national group. Without a doubt, I knew this kind of music was my best mode of expression. It became the focal point of what I wanted to do as a career.

Nonetheless, there was something deeper that was motivating and driving me, though I didn't recognize it at the time. On an outer level, I was looking for fame and fortune just like everyone else. But all along, there was a more subtle and profound force that was driving me, and it was the same thing that caused me to write the kind of songs I was beginning to create. I was getting away from the usual boy-girl songs and replacing them with music and lyrics that explored more complex questions. These songs were unfocused and esoteric at this point, but they were related to philosophical and spiritual issues.

One of these songs was filled with grandiose ideas that really had no center or direction. I called it "Myriad" because it was a product of a myriad of impressions that kept coming into my mind, almost demanding to be expressed. This rather long, elaborate song had no specific message, but I was proud of it because it was the first of that sort that I can recall having written. It had many movements and a broad musical scope that corresponded to the unfocused lyrics. I was trying to convey more of a mood than a message.

I started to title my songs with fictitious words and continued this practice for the next three or four years. "Serenome,"
for example, was the name of one of the songs written during
the Saratoga period. Of course, I had no idea of what this word
meant. Words like this just came into my head, and I wanted
to use them to title the songs to complete the effect of originality
in the lyrics and music. The titles and lyrics were designed to
get the listeners to think and to use their imaginations while
listening to the music. Ironically, if anyone had asked me about
the meaning of some of my lyrics, I would have been at a loss
to answer.

My interest in anything mystical or mysterious kept growing, and I was open to practically any new source of information
to satisfy my appetite. It could be an ancient or modern phenomenon, something I read in a book or saw in a film, or
someone else's drug experience. As long as it had a mystical ring
to it, I was interested. The problem was that I was too uncritical
and often failed to evaluate the possible implications of the
things that were attracting me. I naively thought that everything
in the mystical and spiritual realm was benign. If it enhanced
my visions, images or feelings, I somehow assumed it must be
good.

Fortunately, I did not get involved in the practice of witch-
craft. As undiscerning as I was, I still knew it would be unwise
to get enmeshed in the incantations and spells of "white" magic,
let alone "black" magic. I only dabbled in the world of the
occult, limiting myself to toying with certain forms of divination.
On a number of occasions we played with a Ouija board and
manipulated the planchette to say what we wanted it to say,
usually funny and ridiculous things. This was all very entertain-
ing, but when I was alone with my girlfriend, I decided to see
if it really could say something on its own. Both of us placed our
fingers on the planchette and relinquished all control. Before we
could even ask a question, it took off and immediately said,
"Build me a house." It kept repeating that statement, and we
realized that whatever force was manipulating the marker wanted
a dwelling to inhabit. I believe it was a spirit that wanted to
inhabit me or my girlfriend.

Once when we were in New Orleans, I decided to have my fortune read by twin girls who called themselves the Horoscope Sisters. Their Tarot card readings were intriguing, but not always accurate. They knew that I was in love with a girl I was dating and correctly predicted that our relationship would break up. They also told me that I would be moderately successful in my business, and this turned out to be wrong. But I was mildly impressed that without any prior knowledge, they knew not only my astrological sign, but also that of my girlfriend.

Some of my friends were reading the first two books by Carlos Castaneda, *The Teachings of Don Juan: A Yaqui Way of Knowledge* and *A Separate Reality: Further Conversations with Don Juan*. They tried to relate their drug experiences to the bizarre experiences described by Castaneda as a result of his apprenticeship to a Yaqui Indian sorcerer who called himself don Juan.

Through psychedelic drugs (peyote and a paste made from Jimson weed) provided by don Juan, Castaneda was gradually guided into a separate universe that had its own time, space, laws and logic. It was a world of power where one could read minds, talk with animals, fly, change shape, move objects without touching them, and instantly move to distant locations. This required a radical change in Castaneda's whole conceptual framework, the guidance of a *brujo* (sorcerer), ritually prepared drugs, special dances, positions, and chants, "allies," and spiritual "helpers."

In spite of my interest in altered states of consciousness and the absorbing style of Castaneda's books, I skeptically regarded them as pretentious nonsense. Later, however, I modified this opinion because of my changed perspective on the spiritual dimension of reality.

My world view at this time was in a state of flux. The atheistic humanism of Ayn Rand no longer interested me because it seemed inadequate and reductionistic. I was more interested in the philosophy of the new consciousness and the cosmic evolution of mankind. Perhaps mankind was on the verge of a new age, ready for the radical leap to the superman idealized by Nietzsche. It was even possible that these transformations were somehow being engineered by an extraterrestrial or even extradimensional intervention in human affairs.

I was confused about the role of God in all this. Would this new consciousness bring our race closer to a spiritual or even divine consciousness? My explorations into mysticism kept telling me there had to be more to reality than the four-dimensional space-time continuum that we call the cosmos. I could not escape the concept of God, but almost imperceptibly my concept of the divine was moving through a gradual metamorphosis. The new philosophies my friends and I were encountering through our involvement with the drug culture were profoundly influenced by Eastern religious systems.

All this fascinated me, but I didn't know what to align myself with or what I really believed. In the recesses of my mind, I knew there had to be some ultimate basis for meaning and purpose in life, some true source of satisfaction for the inner longing I often felt.

THE QUEST
LEADS TO THE EAST

The period from 1970-77 was a particularly turbulent time for me. During these years, I went from one philosophy to another, from friend to friend, from band to band, and from rags to riches. Propelling myself through diverse life-styles, I seemed to ping-pong back and forth between different gurus, authors and conflicting religious philosophies. All these elements combined to shape my evolving musical style and world view.

My highly impressionable mind kept trying to make sense out of this heterogeneous input, and I actively looked for different levels of validity in otherwise opposing viewpoints. I started to develop an amalgamation of all the things I took in. All of them keenly affected me because each seemed to contain certain elements of truth. I concluded that the areas of conflict were due to distortions and limitations in the revelatory process. In this way, I became a real syncretist, fusing elements from many sources, convinced that all of this revelation ultimately sprang from one source. As it filtered down through the wide diversity of races, institutions and cultures, this clear light was diffused and absorbed. Though I believed that all truth came from one source, I was unable to identify that source or determine how I personally related to him or it.

I became a voracious reader, incessantly devouring books and soaking them up like a sponge. Sometimes when I finished reading a book I would think, "Wow, I've really found something that hits the nail right on the head." And then I'd read something else and think, "Well, this also seems to be true, but it's different." The things I selected from each book were like patches that I tried to sew together in an enormous conceptual crazy quilt.

Many of these ideas were tied into the philosophies of the East, part of the trend of the late sixties and early seventies. The books of Hermann Hesse and Alan Watts revolved around these Eastern themes and prepared me for my first undiluted dose of Eastern religion. This came in the form of a book called *Be Here Now*. From there I moved into Zen through the books of D. T. Suzuki. But I did not limit myself to one particular tradition within Eastern religion. As I read books by Sri Chinmoy, Paramahansa Yogananda, Ramana Maharshi, Krishnamurti, and others, I found myself attracted to many facets of Hinduism, Buddhism and Taoism.

I never became much of a meditator, however, because I could not subject my will to a completely empty state of mind. I read repeatedly how I had to purify my mind to merge with the one consciousness, but I could never do that. In the back of my mind, which refused to go blank, I always maintained a self-awareness. There was an undercurrent that I could not eradicate, and I struggled with the concept of erasing my own personality.

My world view was eclectic, composed of various elements drawn from the East and the West. But there was one figure who never seemed to blend in. Somehow I was never satisfied with the many attempts I read to fit Jesus Christ into the picture. The best I could do was file him away in a compartment in the back of my mind under the label of an extraordinary guru or messenger from God. I didn't read the Bible during these years, and at one point I decided that if Christ was some sort of a great revealer of divine truth, I owed it to myself to read the New Testament accounts about him. So I started to read the Gospels and went through Matthew and halfway through Mark before deciding to stop. This was a confusing rather than a clarifying experience, because it didn't mesh with the rest of my input.

For awhile, I was quite a Hermann Hesse fanatic. His novels portrayed a search for a unified vision of life that transcends the traditional systems of morality. Absolute reality for him was beyond rationality, values or meaning. I read *Rosshalde* and *Narcissus and Goldmund,* but these themes emerged more clearly in *Siddhartha, Steppenwolf,* and *The Journey to the East.*

Siddhartha (1922) explores the spiritual pilgrimage of a young Indian contemporary of Buddha as he searches for the purpose of human existence. *Steppenwolf,* written in 1927, contrasts the decadent post-war European society with the spirit-realm of "The Immortals." This book was particularly popular at the time I read it because of its psychedelic Magic Theater and spiritual imagery. Man's true search, according to this novel, is for the eternal:

> The communion of the saints, in earlier times it was set by painters in a golden heaven, shining, beautiful and full of peace, and it is nothing else but what I meant a moment ago when I called it eternity. It is the kingdom on the other side of time and appearances. It is there we belong. There is our home. It is that which our heart strives for. . . . For the first time I understand Goethe's laughter, the laughter of the immortals. It was a laughter without an object. It was simply light and lucidity. It was that which is left over when a true man has passed through all the sufferings, vices, mistakes, passions and misunderstandings of men and got through to eternity and the world of space. And eternity was nothing else than the redemption of time, its return to innocence, so to speak, and its transformation again into space.[1]

Hesse's symbolic autobiography, *The Journey of the East,* also involves the pursuit of a timeless spiritual realm. This realm cannot be described in rational terms since it is beyond the space-time categories. Because of this, its narrator is unable to communicate the chronicle of his journey:

> Our Journey to the East and our League, the basis of our community, has been the most important thing, indeed the only important thing in my life, compared with which my own individual life has appeared completely unimportant. And now that I want to hold fast to and describe this most important thing, or at least something

of it, everything is only a mass of separate fragmentary pictures which has been reflected in something, and this something is myself, and this self, this mirror, whenever I have gazed into it, has proved to be nothing but the uppermost surface of a glass plane. I put my pen away with the sincere intention and hope of continuing tomorrow or some other time, or rather to begin anew, but at the back of my intention and hope, at the back of my really tremen-dous urge to relate our story, there remains a dreadful doubt. . . . This doubt does not only ask the question, "Is your story capable of being told?" It also asks the question, "Was it possible to experience it?"[2]

Magister Ludi (The Glass Bead Game) was Hesse's last novel (1943), and it won him the Nobel Prize. This was by far his most difficult and complex work, and unfortunately it was the first Hesse book I read. But I soon came to appreciate this subtle masterpiece, and a number of the spiritual concepts in it deeply affected my thinking.

My first direct exposure to Eastern philosophy came from *Be Here Now,* published in 1971 by the Lama Foundation. The first part is an autobiographical account of the transformation of Dr. Richard Alpert (formerly an associate of Timothy Leary) into Baba Ram Dass. The core book, printed on brown paper, is called "From Bindu to Ojas." This section contains a number of illustrated thoughts that communicate the philosophy of Hin-duism in very simple terms. One of these concerns the hidden self, the *atman:*

> And what is this place?
> Hindus call it the atman
> And what is the atman?
> The Bhagavadam, one of the holy books of India says:
> The atman or divine self
> Is separate from the body
> It is one
> Without a second
> Pure, self-luminous
> Without attributes
> Free

All-pervading
It is the eternal witness
Blessed is he who knows this atman
For, though an embodied being
He shall be free
From the changes and qualities
Pertaining to the body
He alone is ever united with me

This is the place of pure being
That inner place where you dwell
You just be. There is nothing to be
Done in that place. From that place
Then, it all happens, it manifests in
Perfect harmony with the universe.
Because you are the laws of the universe
You are the laws of the universe![3]

This book teaches the unity of all religions and peoples and stresses the need to discover the divine within. Another section, called "Cookbook for a Sacred Life," is a manual designed to get Western readers into the actual practice of Hinduism through Karma and Bhakti Yoga, meditation and chanting of mantras, study, renunciation, purification and so forth.

Be Here Now teaches that there are many paths to enlightenment. Some are faster, some are slower, but all ultimately lead in the same direction. I wanted to get on one of those paths, and I decided to read more about them.

The writings of D. T. Suzuki (e.g., *Essays in Zen Buddhism, Studies in Zen*) provided my introduction to Zen Buddhism. The adherents of Zen seek to penetrate the barriers of language and rationality in order to achieve the intuitive flash of *satori*. Through deep meditation (*zazen*) and the use of irrational problems (*koans*) designed to baffle the mind of the meditator, the Zen master seeks to overcome the shackles of reason in his pupils and lead them to enlightenment. Suzuki writes:

According to the philosophy of Zen, we are too much of a slave to the conventional way of thinking, which is dualistic through and through. No "interpenetration" is allowed, there takes place no fusing of opposites in our everyday logic. . . . Zen, however, upsets this scheme of thought and substitutes a new one in which there exists no logic, no dualistic arrangement of ideas. . . . Where then is the ground of non-dualism on which the soul can be really and truthfully tranquil and blessed? To quote Eckhart again, "Simple people conceive that we are to see God as if He stood on that side and we on this. It is not so; God and I are one in the act of my perceiving Him." In this absolute oneness of things Zen establishes the foundations of its philosophy.[4]

The Gospel According to Zen was particularly fascinating to me because of its attempt to synthesize the religious philosophies of the East and West. In the first chapter, Erich Fromm made this claim: "Zen Buddhism helps man to find an answer to the question of his existence, an answer which is essentially the same as that given in the Judeo-Christian tradition. . . ."[5] Any differences are eliminated by saying that God is beyond theology. "The final meaning of negative theology, of knowing God by unknowing, of the abandonment of idols both sensible and conceptual, is that ultimate faith is not in or upon anything at all. It is complete letting go."[6]

Nevertheless, the issue of theology cannot be avoided, and Zen teaches that there is no personal God. "Zen demonstrates the nullity of all belief in a personal God, and the deplorable constraint that necessarily flows from this belief. It says: 'Do not put any head above your own'; it says also: 'Search not for the truth; only cease to cherish opinions.' "[7]

The portrait of Jesus in this book was very different from anything I had ever heard before, and I was surprised by some of the sayings attributed to him. For example:

> Jesus said:
>   I am the light
>   which is over everything.
>   I am the All;
>   from me the All has gone forth,
>   and to me the All has returned.
>   Split wood: I am there.
>   Lift up the stone, and you will find me there.[8]

It was only later that I discovered that he never said these things in the Gospels. The words of Jesus were either deliberately fabricated or given absurd interpretations to make his teachings fit those of Zen. This troubled me when I realized this years later.

The books of Alan Watts, one of the contributors to *The Gospel According to Zen,* were popular at this time; so I read a few of them. *The Way of Zen* impressed me because of its clear and comprehensive explanation of the history, philosophy and impact of Zen Buddhism. In *Beyond Theology,* Watts attempted to debunk the way Christianity takes itself so seriously and argued that we must break away from theological models to experience our unity with the cosmos. By 1964, twenty years after his ordination as an Anglican priest, Watts had completely abandoned Christianity for pantheism:

> . . . a superior religion goes beyond theology. It turns toward the center; it investigates and feels out the inmost depths of man himself, since it is here that we are in most intimate contact, or rather, in *identity* with existence itself. Dependence on theological ideas and symbols is replaced by direct, non-conceptual *touch* with a level of being which is simultaneously one's own and the being of all others. For at the point I am most myself I am most beyond myself.[9]

Another book along these lines that influenced my thinking was *The Inner Promise,* a compendium of Sri Chinmoy's teachings on the attainment of inner perfection. Chinmoy teaches that "Spirituality tells man that he is God veiled and that God is man revealed."[10] Through the self-discipline of Yoga we can achieve a state of purity which will bring us into union with the supreme source of all being. "Yoga and life are as inseparable as the Creator and the Creation."[11]

Like other Hindu teachers, Sri Chinmoy asserts the unity of all religions by reinterpreting them in Hinduistic terms:

> Unfortunately there is a slight difference between your approach to God and my approach to God. Do you remember what the Son of God said to humanity? He said,

"I and my Father are one." I believe in the Son of God.
I try to live this truth. I also believe in our Vedic seers of
the hoary past. They said, "Brahmasmi"—"I am the Brahman. I am the One without a second." I also have implicit
faith in Sri Krishna's teaching, which I have learned from
his *Gita,* the Song Transcendental: "A man is made by his
faith. Whatever his faith is, so is he."

Sri Krishna is Illumination Incarnate. The Buddha is
Liberation Incarnate. The Christ is Salvation Incarnate.

The world is offering its Darkness to Sri Krishna. The
world is offering its Suffering to the Buddha. The world is
offering its Sin to the Christ.[12]

God is both the One and the Many in Eastern thought. On earth,
he is manifested in multiplicity like a lotus with innumerable
petals.[13] Chinmoy teaches that we have journeyed from mineral
life to plant life and then to the animal kingdom. The journey
of successive reincarnations has brought us to the level of humanity, but it will not be over until we have become divine
beings. We must ultimately be transformed into God himself to
complete the circle.

Each incarnation is leading us toward a higher life,
a better life. We are in the process of evolution. Man is
progressing consciously and unconsciously. But if he makes
progress in each incarnation consciously, then he is ex-
pediting his spiritual progress. Realization will take place
much sooner for him than for those who are making progress
unconsciously.[14]

I was quite taken with Claudio Naranjo's *The One Quest*
because he seemed to successfully amalgamate the whole range
of ancient and modern approaches to the raising of consciousness and self-actualization. As a psychologist in sympathy with
the Esalen Institute, Naranjo argued that the true quest of religion, education and psychiatry is the realization of the true Self.

. . . the distinction between Man and God is also reab-
sorbed into unity, whether this is expressed in theistic or
nontheistic language. In the former case it is expressed as
being one with God or part of God, and in the latter the

feelings that are usually "projected" in a God image or concept are reincorporated in the world and in man. In this way, too, Man is God, the experience of Self becomes endowed with the quality of sanctity, profoundness, ineffability, and especially with that of being an end in itself.[15]

The One Quest, like so many other books I was reading at this time, taught that, rightly interpreted, the great religious teachers of all epochs were really saying the same thing:

> The process of which we are speaking is at the heart of the so-called mystical death and rebirth, in which the outer man ceases to be and the inner man is born. The "death" aspect of it is conveyed by the Buddhistic nirvana (meaning "extinction," and signifying also a transcendence of death); by the Christian "death in Christ," and by the Moslem *fanā-f'illah* (extinction into God). The rebirth aspect is implied in all of these, for nirvana is conceived as mukti (liberation and extinction of individuality in God) which means the recognition that God is what we truly are, while we deceive ourselves into believing that we are our individual masks. Our true being is "Christ in us" (Saint Paul). Every human being is the Buddha, without knowing it. Though the word *rebirth* is true to the quality of the experience, its nature is more that of an awakening to the realization of the nature of the self.[16]

I also read J. Krishnamurti's *Think on These Things,* another book that stressed the liberation of the self, although from a different perspective. Many of Krishnamurti's teachings were more along the lines of Zen than Hinduism because he refused to be systematic or even consistent in his approach.[17] He eschewed adherence to any scheme of religious dogma: "If you hold firmly to some set of beliefs or other, you look at everything through that particular prejudice or tradition; you don't have any contact with reality."[18] He later added, ". . . if a man is seeking God he shuns temples because they divide people. The Christian church, the Mohammedan mosque, your own Hindu temple—they all divide people, and a man who is seeking God will have none of these things."[19]

In *The Spiritual Teaching of Ramana Maharshi,* I read Maharshi's answers to a series of questions raised by a disciple concerning mind control, self-realization, self and individuality, and so forth. Like other gurus, Maharshi taught that "The Self itself is the world; the Self itself is 'I'; the Self itself is God; all is Siva, the Self."[20] But the veil of the ego must be removed before one can come to the final state of realization of the true Self. It was in this way that Maharshi reinterpreted the crucifixion of Christ:

> The body is the cross. Jesus, the son of man, is the ego or "I-am-the-body"-idea. When the son of man is crucified on the cross, the ego perishes, and what survives is the Absolute Being. It is the resurrection of the Glorious Self, of the Christ—the Son of God.[21]

Another Eastern work that moved me was the *Tao Teh Ching* of Lao Tsze. This sixth-century B.C. Chinese philosopher penned a small manuscript of 5,000 characters in his old age just before his retirement into seclusion. This little book changed the course of Chinese philosophy, because it became the central scripture of Taoism. Here are four of the many stanzas that captured my imagination:

> Yet only God's self can impart
>   Completion to the soul,
> And some day every human heart
>   Shall comprehend the whole.
>
> Sustained by earth, encompassed round
>   By heaven serene and pure;
> And yet it is the soundless sound
>   That renders all secure.
>
> Perfection is not yet complete,
>   Or all would cease to be;
> Yet, even then, all would repeat
>   Throughout eternity.
>
> A man must differ to be great;
>   What greatness is expressed
> By him who shares the common fate,
>   And follows all the rest?[22]

The last of these stanzas was so important to me that I framed it and used it as a motto.

I also studied the *I Ching*[23] or *Book of Changes* because it was an outgrowth of Taoist philosophy. The Tao or "way" is the primal cause of the cosmos, the unity that gave birth to the world of opposites. The Yin-Yang philosophy of the *I Ching* stands behind the body of sixty-four hexagrams that is consulted as an oracle to discern the proper course of action in any given situation.

Thaddeus Golas wrote an unusual book called *The Lazy Man's Guide to Enlightenment*. This little volume dealt with various states of consciousness and built upon the thesis that "We are equal beings and the universe is our relations with each other. The universe is made of one kind of entity: each one is alive, each determines the course of his own existence."[24] I was attracted by the elusive nature of this book because it seemed to tie a lot of religious threads together without getting entangled in any of them.

Passages About Earth by William Irwin Thompson was considerably more profound and forced me to do some hard thinking. His impressive analysis of history, contemporary culture, science and religion led him to the conclusion that we are on the verge of a new planetary culture that will emerge through the creation of a collective consciousness. One of the decisive themes in this book is that twentieth-century Western physics and Eastern philosophy are asserting similar things about the nature of the cosmos. He writes:

> Nature is spirit which does not have the appearance of spirit for those perceiving it diachronically; for those perceiving it synchronically in the consciousness of samadhi, nature is once again spirit. Mass, energy, and consciousness are seen to be a single continuum and not a broken universe of real objective events and unreal subjective thoughts.[25]

Without going into his jargon, Thompson is saying that in the final analysis the spiritual realm cannot be avoided because it is all around us. He predicts that "an evolutionary transformation of human culture"[26] will soon take place that will bring us into greater collective conformity with that primary unifying principle.

Not surprisingly, this book argues that traditional or exoteric forms of Western religion are completely inadequate for this new planetary transformation:

> It is sad to think how little of the esoteric has survived in Christianity, and how we must go the whole length of the world to find something as simple as a breathing technique for quieting the mind so that we may enter states of consciousness deeper than the exoteric prayers of give-me-this and give-me-that. Americans have to go to the "New Religions" because our old religions of Catholic, Protestant, and Jew can give us only the institutional culture of religion and not the experience of God.[27]

Of all the things I read, I suppose the one that affected me most deeply was *Autobiography of a Yogi* by Paramahansa Yogananda. This nearly 600-page book moved beyond theory into practice; it was the story of a real person and his religious experiences. Yogananda was sent by his spiritual master Sri Yukteswar in 1920 to bring spiritual illumination to the West. Here he established the ongoing Self-Realization Fellowship and taught Kriya Yoga until his death in 1952. This form of Yoga was taught in nineteenth-century India by Lahiri Mahasaya, Yogananda's guru's guru. It is a yogic technique "whereby the sensory tumult is stilled, permitting man to achieve an ever-increasing identity with cosmic consciousness."[28]

I was astounded by Yogananda's accounts of visions, telepathic communications, and materializations of gurus before and after their deaths. On one occasion while he was in Serampore, his guru Sri Yukteswar, away in Calcutta, suddenly materialized before him:

> "I was pleased that you got my telepathic message." . . .
> As I still stared mutely, Sri Yukteswar went on, "This is not an apparition, but my flesh and blood form. I have been divinely commanded to give you this experience, rarely known on earth." . . .

My guru placed both hands on my head, with a murmured blessing. As he concluded with the words, *"Tabe asi,"* I heard a peculiar rumbling sound. His body began to melt gradually within the piercing light. First his feet and legs vanished, then his torso and head, like a scroll being rolled up. To the very last, I could feel his fingers resting lightly on my hair. The effulgence faded; nothing remained before me but the barred window and a pale stream of sunlight.[29]

Even more overwhelming to me was Yogananda's account of the "resurrection" of both his guru and his guru's guru, Lahiri Mahasaya. Mahasaya appeared after his death to a disciple, and Yukteswar appeared after his death to Yogananda. This struck a chord very deep within me because it was the first time I had run across a resurrection like that of Christ in any of my religious studies.

Keshabananda, a disciple of Mahasaya, told Yogananda about his master's postmortem materialization to him:

" 'I am going home.'
"Our sobs of anguish broke out like an irresistible torrent.
" 'Be comforted; I shall rise again.' After this utterance Lahiri Mahasaya rose from his seat, thrice turned his body around in a circle, assumed a lotus posture while facing the north, and gloriously entered *mahasamadhi.*
"Lahiri Mahasaya's beautiful body, so dear to the devotees, was cremated with solemn householder rites at Manikarnika Ghat by the holy Ganges," Keshabananda continued. "The following day, at ten o'clock in the morning, while I was still in Banaras, my room was suffused with a great light. Lo! before me stood the flesh and blood form of Lahiri Mahasaya. It looked exactly like his old body, except that it appeared younger and more radiant. My divine guru spoke to me.
" 'Keshabananda,' he said, 'it is I. From the disintegrated atoms of my cremated body, I have resurrected a remodeled form.' "[30]

As I read this, I was flying to Atlanta to visit a girlfriend. The idea of this man's guru being resurrected literally moved me to tears. There on the plane, I made a vague sort of commitment. I didn't know to whom or to what, but I wanted to know and serve such a guru.

The more I read this book, the more I thought I had found the expression of what I was searching for. I accepted Yogananda's claim that the true teachings of Christ conformed to the true teachings of Hinduism. He compared the Father, Son and Holy Spirit to the *Sat, Tat* and *Aum* in the Hindu scriptures; the Father is the "Absolute, Unmanifested" beyond creation, the Son is the "Christ Consciousness" within creation, and the Spirit is the "outward manifestation of the omnipresent Christ Consciousness."[31] He also asserted that Christ was one of a number of avatars:

> Great prophets like Christ and Krishna come to earth
> for a specific and spectacular purpose; they depart as soon
> as it is accomplished. Other avatars, like Babaji, undertake
> work that is concerned more with the slow evolutionary
> progress of man during the centuries than with any one
> outstanding event of history. Such masters always veil them-
> selves from the gross public gaze and have the power to
> become invisible at will.[32]

Yogananda regarded Babaji as a deathless guru, the "Yogi-Christ of modern India."[33] This *Mahavatar* (Great Avatar) was the guru of Lahiri Mahasaya himself and even appeared to Yogananda.

Later, when I was in Los Angeles, I visited the headquarters of the Self-Realization Fellowship and talked with a few of the people. I also purchased and studied some other books by Yogananda, including *The Science of Religion*. But my commitment to this approach was to be short-lived; something kept me from plunging all the way in.

Another autobiography that influenced me was that of Mohandas K. Gandhi (*An Autobiography: The Story of My Experiments with Truth*). In it, he graphically related his spiritual experiments in his attempt to achieve *moksha*, the liberation from the wheel of successive incarnations. Gandhi was best known for his political and humanitarian achievements, but all these were secondary to his spiritual pursuits.

Jack Kerouac's *On the Road* and *The Dharma Bums* transported me into the subculture that gave birth to my own. The outer and inner journeys of the characters in these novels gave me some understanding of why Zen came to be the dominant spirituality of the beat generation.

Along similar lines, 1974 saw the publication of Robert M. Pirsig's brilliant novel, *Zen and the Art of Motorcycle Maintenance.* This autobiographical excursion into the depths of human consciousness to discover meaning, value and identity enthralled me. Pirsig's search for the meaning of "quality" led to a complex chain of reasoning that ultimately challenged the idea of reason itself. He elevated quality above the normal distinctions of subject and object, classical and romantic, technological and artistic, and made it equivalent to the concept of the Tao or the Buddha. His Zen-like meditations on the nonvalidity of conventional rationality drove him insane. After electric shock treatments, Pirsig tried to reconstruct the thought processes of his pre-shock self (whom he called "Phaedrus") during a motorcycle excursion from Minnesota to California. This time, however, he would carefully avoid the conceptual vortex that had previously swallowed his rationality.

Nikos Kazantzakis, author of *Zorba the Greek,* also wrote an autobiographical novel. *Report to Greco,* written in the winter of his life, records the spiritual anguish of a man who tried to make some sense out of the riddle of reality. I was deeply moved by this "journey of a man with his heart in his mouth, ascending the rough, unaccommodating mountain of his destiny."[34]

Kazantzakis reached the conclusion that God is behind the symbols of all religions:

> I was astonished. "What—are you praying?" I asked him.
>
> "Of course I am praying, my young friend. Every race and every age gives God its own mask. But behind all the masks, in every age and every race, is always the same never-changing God."
>
> He fell silent, but after a moment: "We have the cross as our sacred sign; your most ancient ancestors had the double-edged axe. But I push aside the ephemeral

symbols and discern the same God behind both the cross and the double-edged axe, discern Him and do obeisance."[35]

This concept is rooted in the even more fundamental assertion of the ultimate unity of all things. The following passage has a very Eastern ring to it:

> "By means of this awareness of self, man was separated from God. Originally everything was united with God, contented in His bosom. There was no such thing as you, me, and him, no such thing as yours and mine; there were not two, there was one. One cosmos, one Being. This was the paradise you hear about, this and only this. From here we all had our start. This is what the soul remembers; to this it longs to return. Blessed be death!"[36]

Like the sages of Hinduism, Kazantzakis saw the ego as the only barrier between man and God.[37] The struggle between the man and God within each of us is really the struggle between the flesh and the spirit. *Report to Greco* portrays Christ as the model of the human soul's sacrificial ascent to indissoluble union with God:

> Following Christ's bloody tracks, we must fight to transubstantiate the man inside us into spirit, so that we may merge with God.
> This dual nature of Christ had always been a deep, inscrutable mystery to me, and especially the yearning, so human, so superhuman, of Christ the man to attain to God, or, more exactly, to return to God and become identical with Him.[38]

So many of the books I read during these years attempted to blend the person of Christ into conformity with their contradictory systems. The inevitable result was a series of contradictory Christs, none of whom resembled the Christ of the Bible. One of the most extreme distortions I came across was in *Seth Speaks,* a book that was dictated through the "borrowed" body of Jane Roberts, a spirit-medium. A spirit-being who called himself Seth

first began to communicate with her when she was experiment-
ing with a Ouija board. Subsequently, she frequently fell into
trance states as she allowed Seth to control her body and speak
through her mouth. In this book, Seth claimed that Christ actually consisted of three separate personalities, and that the third
has yet to appear (the "second coming"). He also denied the
crucifixion and maintained that Christ was simply "a great psy-
chic."[39]

Seth rejected the existence of evil and said through Ruburt
(his name for Jane Roberts) that "there are no devils or demons,
except as you create them out of your belief. . . . good and evil
effects are basically illusions."[40] Furthermore, God is only an
idea that was projected out of man's emerging ego.[41] Thus, truth
cannot be "found by going from teacher to teacher, church to
church, or discipline to discipline, but by looking within the
self."[42] I later came to suspect that the spirit who was possessing
Jane Roberts was not benign but demonic.

One of the reasons I read *Seth Speaks* was because Richard
Bach praised it as one of the best books he had ever read.[43] I
had previously read his *Jonathan Livingston Seagull*, a thinly veiled
popular allegory of Hinduistic philosophy. In it, a spiritually
receptive seagull breaks away from the shackles of materialism,
and with the help of a guru named Chaing learns to transcend
the boundaries of space and time as he becomes aware of the
limitlessness of his true nature.[44] He then returns to earth almost
like an avatar to lead other seagulls into this knowledge. At this
point, Bach brings in obvious analogies to Christ, and Jonathan
Livingston Seagull comes to be regarded as a "Son of the Great
Gull"[45] prior to his glorious departure from earth.

My reading in 1970-77 also included a healthy dose of
science fiction. Some of the more intriguing among these SF
books were Arthur C. Clarke's *Childhood's End* and *2001: A Space
Odyssey*, Robert A. Heinlein's *Stranger in a Strange Land*, and
Roger Zelazny's *Lord of Light*. I was also interested in philosophy
(e.g., E. L. Allen, *From Plato to Nietzsche*) and astronomy (e.g.,
*Cosmic Connection: An Extraterrestrial Perspective, In Quest of Quasars,
Other Worlds*, and the controversial *Worlds in Collision* by Veli-
kovsky).

Three books that seemed to be quite different from all the others I encountered in this period were *The Fellowship of the Ring, The Two Towers,* and *The Return of the King,* collectively known as *The Lord of the Rings.* J. R. R. Tolkien's wonderful fantasy trilogy absolutely captivated me. I finished it and immediately read it again. I loved it because of the fascinating characters, skillful writing, and imaginative plot, but there was something special that appealed to me beyond these things. This was a genuine sense of right and wrong, of good and evil. I didn't find this kind of absolute morality in the other things I was reading, especially the books about Eastern religion. The Tolkien trilogy was profoundly satisfying, and though a fantasy it seemed to carry a deeper truth than the books that were claiming to be the truth. I later found out why.

Throughout the time I was trying to synthesize Eastern and Western forms of spirituality and religious philosophy, there was one religious undercurrent that kept flowing. Regardless of what new direction my belief system would take, I continued to develop an intense kind of worship that was centered around music.

Music was capable of affecting me at a deeper level than religious postures, meditation or books. Classical and contemporary music became a crucial input for me, but the need for musical output was even more essential. Music began to take shape not only as an expression of my artistic ideas, but also as an expression of my mystical and religious feelings. The creative process in me that drew from many sources and manifested itself in the writing and production of music became a kind of worship. My concept of deity at this point was vague and remote; I could ascribe no name to it, and it really had no personal form. But I believed it was worthy of worship, and found that the most satisfying way to accomplish this was through the medium of music.

In some vague way, I actually began to elevate this music to the point where it became an object of worship and not just a means of worship. This was a confusing period, and my elastic world view allowed me almost no solid footing.

Appendix to Chapter 4

I selected the following poems to illustrate the metamorphosis in my thinking during the period described in Chapter 4. They were written between 1971 and 1976.

THE CATCH (1971)

Against the wall, their solemn eyes peering
Anticipating the dryness of sun and light
With only a wishing glint as sign of past vigor,
The gaping denizens fade
Beggars surround and approach their ordained duty,
Blind oaths sworn on the cutting board
Ignorant of the lights dimmed by bloody hands,
Cold steel slashes the sunlit array,
And the splay adorns the tide
Gaining the apex of their destiny,
Humble creatures of simplicity,
An untapped source of light and wisdom becomes offal,
Who burn and taint the air

DRIFTING SILENTLY THROUGH SHIMMERING DAYS (1972)

Drifting silently through shimmering days,
Blowing in the winds of fortune's choice,
Who can hear that sweet melody?
I strain against the bonds of time
That hold me from its flowing line
Do my ears alone taste the peace of its solace?

Surround me with your boundless grace,
And take me to that holy place,
Where, unencumbered, I will bask in your light,
And sail unseen on the blind winds of fortune

UNTITLED (1973)

Hanging in the balance, waiting for a sway, a sign
Resting in embryonic repose, totally content with
The incompleteness of the moment
The rain (or is it reign) of insanity pounds against
The walls of this absurd shell that encloses my thoughts
Thoughts that helplessly appear on the screen before a
Bored viewer who paid too much to get in

POISED CHROME OVOID (1974)

Motor overdrive wheel wrenches, twisting the thrashing,
bug-eyed pawn
He's brilliant as a poised chrome ovoid in a glass lake
Plotting arrows of fire in the night, they gathered
to observe their offspring in the green darkness of
primeval caves
Chants and arias transpose the flickering shadows
into towering mansions
Slowly turning, the comical statue face charms the
transfixed skyline, titillating his base sense cortex
into spasms of nervous mutation

THE PINNACLE (1975)

I've so much to say, I do not speak
At rest, I consume and absorb
I observe, inanimate, and with insatiable lust
The ways of the innocent
Their frail endeavors sweep me down currents of
vain indulgence, but do not touch me
I long for their empty security, and yet I loathe it

To cover myself with a cloak of awareness,
And turn my eyes away,
To embrace the essence of the Source,
and impress its perfect order on my wandering
        thoughts,
To emanate the purity of its guidance

And welcome all that exists,
To this end I drown my desires in a sea of loneliness,
And stand, isolated, on a pinnacle of hope

SATORI (1976)

In a twilight hour, passing time at rest,
Engulfed was I in sweet atonement
A roaring silence swirled past my ears,
And that which sees beyond was in my eyes

I chose to wed the moment, one sanctioned with
    wonder,
My soul rose on wings of gold and soared through
    amber skies
Lost in clouds of singing voices,
Sweet tears of bliss were borne on scented breezes
To alight in the brilliant sea of their origin
Celestial music surrounded me with unbearable
    movement

I am not I, for I am all, a blinding light
The heavens part for my passing, and I reel with the
Thunder of God
I burst into galaxies of fulfillment
My soul draws within itself, a point of pure being

I am the babe, and the gasp of the dying
At one with all, I surrender to the eternity of the
    moment

CREDO (1976)

First know that I have the Love. I trace my thought
in symbols and signs for you to know, though you know
it already. I am inside you, looking out through your eyes,
breathing your breath, thinking your thoughts. Though
you hide behind the wall you built, it will crumble and you
will be free of the bonds of flesh. You are afraid of the very
thing you long for, and you flee your nameless home.
    Come to me, and know the meaning which is no

meaning. I thought that I was here, just as you are sure you are reading these words. Illusion. There is no death when there is nothing to die. There is no need of words to tell you of emptiness. I remember, and somewhere you remember. You and I and all of us, all that lives, will learn enough and feel enough that we will go home. Do you understand that there is boundless joy? Boundless and without end! All the grandeur and love and beauty and light are waiting. They were here all the time. Sometimes we glimpse it for a second and shed a tear, but we are not strong enough to let go, to surrender all. Even as I know this, I cling to my life. Even as you read this you understand in that place where I am inside you, but what you think you are will not let go. We all search for God. Why do we look outside for what is in? WE ARE GOD.

MUSICAL INFLUENCES

Just as my reading dramatically reshaped my world view, so the hundreds of records I listened to profoundly affected my developing musical style. This musical input really began in grammar school when, as I mentioned earlier, my fourth grade teacher played a number of classical selections for us. My Aunt Lily deepened this exposure during the hours we spent together listening to and talking about the music of Bach, Handel, Beethoven, Mendelssohn, Schumann, Chopin, Franck, Brahms, Tchaikovsky, and other composers. So much of this music enriched my imagination and left a permanent mark on the kind of musical style I would later develop.

The organ music at my church gave me a love for baroque music, especially that of Bach. I also enjoyed a very different kind of music when I went to see films like *Journey to the Center of the Earth, The 7th Voyage of Sinbad, The Day the Earth Stood Still,* and *Fahrenheit 451*. The music in these movies evoked a sense of adventure and mystery, and successfully created the impression of other worlds. It was not until years later that I discovered that the scores of all four of these films were written by the same composer, Bernard Herrmann (this was in 1974 when I bought a record called *The Fantasy Film World of Bernard Herrmann*).

The symphonic poems of Richard Strauss captivated me in high school, especially the philosophical ones like *Death and Transfiguration* (1889) and *Thus Spoke Zarathustra* (1896). The former depicted the convulsions of a dying man and the liberation of his soul through death. The latter was a highly symbolic commentary on the philosophy of Friedrich Nietzsche. I already described the impact Stanley Kubrick's film *2001: A Space Odyssey* had on me. Strauss' *Thus Spoke Zarathustra* was its predominant theme, and I listened to the record of the sound track over and over. The Adagio from Aram Khachaturian's *Gayane Ballet Suite* was also on the sound track, and this poignant music enchanted me.

Richard Wagner was one of my favorite composers, and the sound from his music dramas, like *Tannhäuser* (1845), *Lohengrin* (1850), *Die Walküre* (1857), *Götterdämmerung* (1874), and *Parsifal* (1882), bowled me over. I loved the way he wove leitmotifs into his music and delighted in his use of elaborate chromatic chord progressions and sudden changes of key.

There are a number of other compositions that engaged me in these years. I loved *Peer Gynt* (1875), Edvard Grieg's incidental orchestral music to Henrik Ibsen's play, because it had a spirit of adventure, fantasy and mystery about it. These same qualities were also in Nicolai Rimsky-Korsakov's beautiful symphonic suite of scenes from the *Arabian Nights, Scheherazade* (1888). This and Antonin Dvořák's Symphony No. 9, "From the New World" (1893), had the power to waft me off into an altogether different world. This kind of music seemed to reach inside me and create a sense of longing for something I couldn't name. Along these lines I also treasured Modest Mussorgsky's *Pictures at an Exhibition* (1874) as orchestrated by Maurice Ravel (1922) and the music of Claude Debussy, particularly *Prelude to the Afternoon of a Faun* (1894), *Nocturnes* (1899), *La Mer* (1905), and his first book of *Préludes* (1910; especially *The Girl with the Flaxen Hair* and *The Engulfed Cathedral*). Debussy's impressionistic music used a rich range of harmonic color effects to create an atmosphere of enchantment, not unlike the "long ago and far away" of well-crafted fairy tales.

This same pastoral serenity abounds in Samuel Barber's *Adagio for Strings* (1936). As many times as I have played this *Adagio,* it never fails to overpower me. "The music has a faintly archaic air: it is an essay in austere polyphony, slowly rising in dynamic intensity through a series of lingering chordal suspensions leading to languorous cadences."[1] This music is reminiscent of an earlier piece of music that also enthralled me, *Adagio for Strings and Organ* by the Venetian baroque composer Tomaso Albinoni.

The music of Ralph Vaughan Williams also influenced me, and this was especially true of *The Lark Ascending* (1920). This exquisite composition, along with other works like *Fantasia on a Theme of Thomas Tallis* (1909) and *Job* (1931), made me imagine a world better than the one I was living in.

On a very different note, one of the most powerful musical experiences I ever had was in 1975 when I first heard Gustav Mahler's greatest work, *Symphony of a Thousand* (Symphony No. 8; 1906-07). This monumental symphony, based on Goethe's *Faust,* depicted the spiritual themes of judgment and redemption. I wept at the denouement when the mystical choir sang, "Look up, all creatures frail and contrite! . . . All things transitory are but parable; here insufficiency becomes fulfillment, here the indescribable is accomplished. . . ."[2]

Thus, the music that most affected me took two forms: beautiful and peaceful compositions that captured and transported my imagination, and powerful works that soared into majestic heights of exultation.

These classical influences have often surfaced in my music. I chose the genre of rock music for my compositions, but gradually modified it in an attempt to synthesize some aspects of classical and rock.

Over the years I became familiar with the music of hundreds of rock bands, and some of them have indelibly stamped my musical style. I'll only list the groups and records that were most significant to me.

In the early sixties I was strongly attracted to the music of The Kinks and The Yardbirds because they played a harder brand of rock than anyone at that time. I was totally into Yardbird albums like *For Your Love, Rave Up,* and *Over Under Sideways Down,* and patterned my early rock style after them.

The period from 1966 to 1971 was really the heyday of creative rock music, and the groups that most influenced me flourished during those years. There is no special order to the following albums except that most of them fit into this period.

Procol Harum made a major impact on me. When I heard their albums *Procol Harum* and *Shine On Brightly,* I felt that they were everything I wanted to be musically at that time rolled up in one ball. Their lyrics were mysterious, sometimes eerie, and their songs dealt a lot with life and death. Their music also displayed a fair amount of classical influence (this was especially evident in "Repent Walpurgis").

A second group that powerfully affected me conceptually and musically was Touch. These excellent musicians created a very big sound, and their music and lyrics were quite original. I especially liked "Down at Circes Place" and "Seventy-five."

Another big influence was King Crimson, particularly *In the Court of the Crimson King.* Their music had a majestic quality, and this was one of the first rock groups that had an orchestral sound. Like Touch, King Crimson was highly original. The poetic lyrics were quite good (e.g., "The Court of the Crimson King, Including The Return of the Fire Witch and the Dance of the Puppets"). Ian McDonald and Michael Giles of King Crimson also produced an interesting album of their own simply titled, *McDonald and Giles.*

Chicago Transit Authority, Chicago's first album, was significant for its unconventional marriage of rhythm and blues with hard rock. I was impressed by the high level of musicianship.

Although it was an obscure group, the esoteric sound of Quatermass also influenced my music.

I admired the powerful rock 'n' roll style of Deep Purple (*Shades of Deep Purple, The Book of Taliesyn*). Their lyrics were cryptic, and they were excellent musicians, especially Richie Blackmore, the lead guitarist.

Eric Clapton of Cream was another fine guitarist. I particularly like Cream's *Disraeli Gears* album.

Like everyone else, I was affected by The Beatles, especially their *Revolver, Rubber Soul,* and *Sgt. Pepper's Lonely Hearts Club Band* albums. They were always on the cutting edge of instrumental and lyrical innovation. I was also interested in the way some of their songs explored Eastern religious subjects. "Tomorrow Never Knows" on *Revolver* begins with words that are reminiscent of the *Tibetan Book of the Dead:*

Turn off your mind,
relax and float downstream
It is not dying
It is not dying

Lay down your thoughts,
surrender to the void
It is shining
It is shining

That you may see
the meaning of within
It is being
It is being[3]

The imagery in some of the songs by The Doors created a strange sensation in me. This was particularly true of "Light My Fire." Jim Morrison's vocals were impressive to me, and some of their songs had very interesting chord changes.

No one before and possibly since (it's hard to say, because he changed everyone) played the guitar like Jimi Hendrix. As a guitarist and as an image-maker, it was as though he had come from another planet. *Are You Experienced?* was brimming with psychedelic images and took me out of the everyday mode of thought.

Pink Floyd (e.g., *Meddle*) had a very innovative quality. They were not spectacular musicians, but they were unusually creative.

Buffalo Springfield was another group with a distinctive style. Their *Buffalo Springfield Again* album had the soaring melodies, harmony and effective chord changes that most groups didn't have. This was especially true of "Expecting to Fly," an exceptionally pretty song.

To me, The Moody Blues were more conceptually than musically significant. They explored mystical subjects in their lyrics, and their Eastern religious orientation was often quite evident. *In Search of the Lost Chord* had a Hindu *yantra* (the visual equivalent of a *mantra*) inside, together with these lines:

Between the eyes and ears there lie,
The sounds of colour,
And the light of a sigh

With thoughts of within
To exclude without
The ghost of a chord
Will expel all doubt

And to name this chord
Is important to some
So they give it a word
And the word is 'OM'[4]

Om is the most sacred word in Hinduism, and it is composed of a humming nasalization of the sounds A, U, M, which represent the triad of gods: Vishnu, Shiva and Brahma.[5]

Eastern religion was also predominant in The Mahavishnu Orchestra with John McLaughlin. *The Inner Mounting Flame,* for instance, inserted a meditation by Sri Chinmoy inside the record sleeve. This album displayed great musicianship.

On a different religious note, The Electric Prunes came up with *Mass in F Minor,* a complete mass in the genre of rock music.

Gentle Giant was one of my favorite groups. Their albums *Three Friends* and *Octopus* had a remarkable originality, good musicianship, and philosophically interesting lyrics. I also had the pleasure of seeing them in concert, and appreciated the energy of their performance.

On the bizarre side, I was attracted by the creativity of Magma, a science fiction band from France. Their music was quite unusual, and they were so obsessed with the idea of being original that they created their own language for the lyrics.

Vangelis, in his album *Heaven and Hell,* very effectively portrayed these spiritual themes with a variety of instruments and synthesizers. Some of the orchestral-sounding music on this album is very beautiful and majestic. (Vangelis more recently created the Oscar-winning score to the superb movie *Chariots of Fire.*)

The albums that follow exerted a minor influence on me. Again, there is no particular order in the way they are listed.

H. P. Lovecraft II was one of those psychedelically-oriented records that used to lead me into that dream world I liked to get into. The Steve Miller Band, especially *Children of the Future,* also had that dreamlike quality. The Grateful Dead and Jefferson Airplane (e.g., *Crown of Creation*) were other innovators during this period.

The Mothers of Invention combined creativity, good musicianship, and a sense of humor. Captain Beefheart had a similar sense of outlandish humor (Frank Zappa produced their *Trout Mask Replica* album). Their lyrics reminded me of some of the crazy poems I was writing during this time. Mad River's *Paradise Bar and Grill* was another unusual album, with songs that seemed to range from the sublime to the ridiculous.

Stonehenge and *Ssssh* by Ten Years After influenced my musicianship more than my thinking. Emerson, Lake & Palmer (e.g., *Tarkus*) created a full sound and made some provocative adaptations of classical music within a rock framework. Another group, Yes, should have been everything I liked, but for some reason they weren't. They made use of esoteric and quasi-religious themes, but they sometimes went so far with their lyrics that it struck me as almost corny. But *The Yes Album, Fragile,* and *Close to the Edge* were musically excellent. Genesis (*Nursery Cryme*) was almost identical to Yes.

I wasn't into The Beach Boys, but there was something about their *Surf's Up* album that I really enjoyed. It evoked a melancholy, sometimes nostalgic feeling. Some of the songs were about the ecological problem (for instance, "A Day in the Life of a Tree"). *Migration* by The Amboy Dukes had good guitar playing and interesting lyrics, some bordering on spiritual issues. *Bee Gee's 1st* had a number of appealing songs, like "Holiday."

Don Ellis' *Tears of Joy* had unusual time signatures, and I emulated some of his arrangements. The first time I heard a rock band use a violin was on the album *It's a Beautiful Day,* and it was used very effectively in the song "Bulgaria." Rhinoceros was the first funky band I liked, primarily because of the style and musicianship. *The Electric Zodiac* was the first album of purely electronic music I heard.

Other somewhat influential albums include: Spirit, *The Family That Plays Together;* The Band, *Music From Big Pink; The Soft Machine;* Small Faces, *There Are But Four Small Faces;* T.I.M.E., *Smooth Ball;* and The Sons of Champlin, *Loosen Up Naturally.*

The last album I'll mention is *Morning Dew.* This Topeka band often worked out in my apartment because the drummer (Don Sligar) was my roommate. Mal Robinson was Morning Dew's songwriter and guitarist, and we decided to write a song together called "Save Me." This song was included in their (1969) album, and it was the first time my name appeared on a record sleeve. Naturally, we were jealous that Morning Dew was making an album and we weren't.

THE THREE KANSAS BANDS

The members of Saratoga were living in my cramped Topeka apartment. The band usually practiced in the back of a local music store after hours. There was practically no market for the kind of original songs we were learning, but we felt impelled to move in this direction. Our kind of music did nothing for Saratoga's local acceptance, and our practice sessions were somewhat clandestine.

During my high school and college years, another Topeka-based group had a rivalry with The Gimlets. This band, called White Clover, moved down to New Orleans to play in various clubs because there was more work down there. Phil Ehart was the drummer for White Clover, and the bass guitarist was Dave Hope. In 1970, Phil was visiting friends in Topeka and heard that a new band called Saratoga was doing original songs. He dropped by the music store, by then the local haunt for musicians, to hear us practice. Apparently he was quite impressed by what he heard; so we started to hang out together at the back of the store.

At first, Phil and I exchanged stories about problems in our respective bands and went over the strengths and weaknesses of all the members. It dawned on us that each group had something the other group needed. Phil's band was short on writers and material, and it was also in need of an excellent lead or second-lead guitarist. I felt we needed a vitality and enthusiasm that some of the members of my band didn't seem to have. So we formulated the idea of selecting the best musicians from Saratoga and White Clover to form a sort of local supergroup.

As we tried to think of a name for the new band, we groped for a title that would reflect where we were from and what we were. We thought it would be wiser to focus on our background rather than concoct some obscure psychedelic name like Chocolate Eyeball. I think it was Dave who finally said, "Why don't we call the band Kansas?"

Kansas didn't strike me as a good name at first, but the more I thought about it, the more appropriate it seemed. It had a clear and original ring to it because few bands at the time were named for geographical places; hence, Kansas was born.

After a few members from both bands were "canned," the rest of White Clover moved back from New Orleans. We really retained too many people, because the new band consisted of eight members. It was almost ridiculous—we seemed to have two of everything. We had two lead singers, because neither band wanted to give up its lead singer. One was a good writer, and the other was a better singer. Everyone went along with this arrangement initially since we thought it would be a novel idea. We also had two keyboard players and two guitar players (a fellow named Larry Baker, who also played saxophone, and me). One of the keyboard players, my friend Don Montre, also played flute while the other, Dan Wright, played a bit of guitar. Thus, we were a real potpourri of the local talent.

Such a strange amalgamation was doomed to experience problems right from the beginning. The two lead singers, of course, were always at odds over who would be the *real* lead in a given song. This problem was resolved at the end of two weeks when the singer from White Clover decided to pack it in. I think we played only one show with the original group of eight.

Kansas became the talk of the town because the best members of two bands that had always been rivals were now all together in one band. Our real debut took place at Domme's Dance Studio on the top floor of an old office building in a decrepit part of downtown Topeka. We plastered posters all over town, and everybody from the "hip" community of Topeka showed up that night. Kansas was on its way.

This first Kansas band was destined to last only a year, but I must say in retrospect that we more than achieved our goal

of originality. Several of us could write songs, but I surfaced as
the main writer of the group. I wrote almost all the music for
that short-lived band, just as I had done for Saratoga. This was
a prolific time for me, and I experimented with a wide variety
of musical forms. It was particularly challenging to write for so
many instruments, and careful orchestration became a necessity
to avoid the otherwise inevitable cacophony and confusion. You
can't take that many musicians who double on different instruments and tell them "One, two, three, go!" So I began to scram-
ble to learn a lot more about music theory and orchestration.
This had a permanent effect on my musical style, which is still
oriented toward orchestration.

The year of the first Kansas band, 1970, was by far the
most bizarre period in my life. We were surrounded by people
who were heavily into drugs, and I was completely immersed
in this culture with all its paraphernalia and patterns. We all
lived in a very communal fashion, and people were continually
coming and going. When we first moved into the house, the
carpet was new and everything was in good order. Immediately
it turned into squalor and filth as band houses are wont to do.
We had animals, frequent guests (some of whom none of us
knew), and stragglers and hitchhikers of all descriptions who had
come into town. It became the scene of every form of hedonism
and the center of the hippie culture in Topeka. This produced
some very interesting happenings, to say the least.

Our band achieved some measure of popularity, but we
were still very poor. We were so unusual that there were really
few places we could play. The only reason club owners would
hire us at all was because they knew we had our own portable
audience that would follow us around. When we played in a
club, we literally took the place over because our followers
would come and pack the place.

It became obvious that we would have to travel to get
enough engagements. We piled our equipment into a big black
school bus and drove all over the Midwest, though most of our
engagements were in the state of Kansas. We would often play
in tiny agricultural towns that had one gas station and a school-
house or perhaps a V.F.W. facility. We put our posters up, and

all the kids from miles around would come to watch the outra-geous band.

The band developed some fairly screwy stage antics, espe-cially in association with a song called "Pandemonium Mass." The song couldn't have been more accurately titled, because it literally led to mass pandemonium. It had a very discordant and unpleasant conclusion which built to a fevered pitch of cacopho-ny. We reacted physically according to the sound of the music with all manner of unrehearsed pranks, frenzied dancing, object throwing, disrobing, and knocking over musical equipment (we couldn't afford to destroy any of it—that takes a certain element of affluence). I remember on one occasion pouring a pitcher of beer over my head and getting shocked half to death as a result.

To add to the whole effect, we dressed very strangely; our poverty caused us to frequent the Salvation Army store where we picked up outlandish outfits for our concerts. We set out to become the most controversial group that had ever hit the Midwest. I think we achieved our goal.

The best example of this kind of activity took place when we were booked to play the 1970 high school prom in Russell, Kansas. Merely the fact that we showed up at this dance was in itself a dichotomy of appearances. We were grubby, dirty, and long-haired, and this was a nice, neat rural high school cotillion; to us, it was like stepping back ten years in time. It was doomed to be a disastrous prom from the very beginning.

We made it a show they would never forget. None of the kids danced through the entire evening; they were standing against the walls of the auditorium staring in disbelief at the spectacle before them. But it all culminated when we started to get into "Pandemonium Mass." Our saxophone player, Larry Baker, put his legs behind his head (he was into yoga), wore a gas mask, and stuck a microphone down his sax. Then he came out from behind the amplifiers, walking on his hands and mak-ing honking noises with the saxophone in his mouth. Girls screamed and ran back in fear of this other-worldly creature. Meanwhile, Lynn Meredith, our lead singer, started tearing down the prom decorations, and the band was roaring at 110 decibels of pure noise. At this point, the high school principal cut our performance short, and a real scene started to erupt when he vehemently refused to pay us. Our head roadie, who hailed from Hawaii (we called him Pineapple), practically got into a fist fight with the principal. I distinctly remember hiding with Dave behind our amplifiers while Pineapple threatened him with a ball-peen hammer. I think we ruined their prom.

Our avowed purpose in this Kansas band was, of course, to record and make it big. I think we were considerably more original than a lot of groups that were recording at that time; our music deserved to be recorded. Perhaps nothing much became of us because we were too bizarre for our surroundings.

Nevertheless, we did have a couple of close calls with success. We ran into a promoter from Denver who called us and said, "I've got you booked at an outdoor pop festival with Deep Purple in Albuquerque, New Mexico." This was in the era of Woodstock and Altamont, and we thought this was the big break we had been looking for. He then told us that in order to pay for the trip (we weren't getting paid for the pop festival) we would have to play for clubs in Denver and Albuquerque. So our whole entourage—guys, girlfriends, roadies, hitchhikers, dogs, equipment—piled into our schoolbus and took off for Denver.

We no sooner left town than I began to feel ill. At first I thought it was just my imagination playing tricks on me; the last thing in the world I wanted was to get sick just as we were leaving for our big break. But I began to get the telltale signs of the flu; so I crawled into the back of the bus and went to sleep on top of the organ. When I woke up, I was delirious with fever. To make matters worse, when we rolled into Denver we found that the place we were booked was called the Pussycat a' Go Go! We took one look at the club and the owner took one look at us and we canceled our booking by mutual agreement.

We went on to Albuquerque, and my condition continued to grow worse. The club was called Poor Richard's (later more aptly named The Muddhole), and we found to our dismay that another band was set up on the stage. The club owner gave us a look of horror as if to say, "What are *you* doing here?" Someone had blundered and the place was double-booked. Since we had driven all the way from Kansas and the other band (called Mudd) was from Albuquerque, he decided to let us play there that week as well. We would set up on the floor in front of Mudd, and both of us would play.

This was better than nothing, because we needed to hang around a week for the pop festival, the real reason we had come down. When we asked where we were going to stay, the owner gave us a blank expression. We said, "We're supposed to be provided with free lodging." So he answered, "OK, get in your bus and follow me."

We drove into a residential neighborhood with nice adobe-type houses. He pulled up in front of a house with the front door standing open and the windows boarded up and told us, "You can stay here, but just don't open the refrigerator."

The house was totally devoid of furniture, and there was no water or electricity. In the kitchen cabinet we found a plastic baggie with cocaine inside, so we concluded that the previous inhabitants had left the house in a hurry. Naturally, we immediately opened up the refrigerator (Dave's curiosity got the best of him), and our suspicions were confirmed. It was an old Crosley refrigerator, and when Dave pulled the handle there was a loud "poof" and a gush of green fog poured out, filling the room with the nauseatingly foul odor of decayed food.

We weren't scheduled to start playing until the next night. So when the others wanted to go down to Poor Richard's to hear Mudd play, I decided to go into one of the bedrooms to recuperate. The room was completely dark because the windows were boarded up. I got into my sleeping bag, and they shut the bedroom door before leaving.

When I woke up, my fever was worse and I was in such a delirium that I totally forgot who I was and where I was. I stood up in utter darkness and began to grope my way along the walls of the room. When I found the door it was locked, and there was no way to escape from the black cubicle. It reminds me of a scene from "The Pit and the Pendulum." I was in a state of complete confusion; my fever was raging, and I was pounding on the walls and screaming. Suddenly the door opened and a flashlight was shining into my eyes. The guys had just returned, and when they shined the flashlight on me I must have looked like a crazed animal.

They calmed me down and helped me remember who and where I was. The next morning when I woke up it was almost as bad. I turned my head and saw two big boots next to my face. I looked up and a man began to yell, "What're you doin' in my house?"

"Uh, uh, we're supposed to stay here."

"I'm gettin' the police."

He ran out of the house, and I stumbled after him trying to get out of my sleeping bag and falling down saying, "Wait! Wait! Don't get the police—we'll leave."

I got all the guys' sleeping bags and suitcases, set them out on the curb, and waited for them to return (I had slept in due to my illness, and the others had gone out for breakfast).

We drove over to the club and found that since we had no money for a hotel, the only place we could sleep was on the floor of the club after the shows. There we were for the rest of the week, sleeping amidst the cigarette butts, beer, and vomit on the dance floor.

Since the club was only a block or two away from the main drag in Albuquerque, we got in the habit of walking over to a Sambo's, a twenty-four-hour restaurant on that street. One night after our show, we were heading over to Sambo's when a girl came running breathlessly across the street. She had short blond hair, tattered jeans, a blue sweatshirt, and she was barefooted. Full of excitement she asked, "Do you want to see the last and greatest of the living Indian chiefs? You've got to come see him."

We said, "Well, . . . OK," and she led our motley entourage across the street and down an alley. A dilapidated Plymouth was parked in the alley, and an old, toothless, drunk Indian was sitting in the back seat.

The girl asked, "Isn't he great?"

"Well, uh, that's pretty amazing . . . we'll see you later." As we started to walk away, this buxom girl suddenly called back to us and lifted up her sweatshirt. The old Indian went into hysterics and we knew it was time to take off.

To our dismay, both of them started following us. We tried

to get rid of them by walking fast, but they caught up to us when Saturday night traffic delayed our crossing the main street. The girl said, "Wait a minute, I'll stop 'em." She walked out on the median, lifted up her sweatshirt, and the cars came to a screeching halt. Meanwhile, we ran across the street and ducked into Sambo's, hoping to have escaped her and the Indian. But the restaurant was brightly lit, and they saw us sitting inside. She walked up to the window, lifted her sweatshirt, and pressed herself against the glass right in front of a guy who was eating in a booth. The Indian was screaming with laughter as she walked in and started to bark like a dog and expose herself. She went up to the man in the booth, and while she barked he calmly tried to eat his steak and eggs as if nothing was wrong. But when she picked up the steak in her teeth and shook it like a dog, he got up and walked out.

She and the Indian calmed down and ate a meal (we stuffed a booth to keep them from joining us). They left before us, and when we got up to pay our bill the girl at the register made us pay for their meal. She explained, "The Indian said you were supposed to pay for them."

Sunday was the day of our big break: the pop festival. Deep Purple was indeed scheduled to play, and we felt that even though everything had been a fiasco so far, this would make it all worthwhile. We got the directions and drove so far out in the desert on a dusty little road that we thought, "This can't be right." Just then, we came over a rise and looked down at thousands of people sitting in the desert in front of a big stage. After parking our bus a long distance from the stage, we walked up to the backstage to find out how we would get our equipment set up. A band named Feather was playing while we were trying to figure out what was going on.

Suddenly I looked up at a long black line coming over the horizon behind the crowd. A cloud of dust was rising from it, and as it drew nearer I realized it was a line of hundreds of motorcycles. The bikers pulled up and a huge fight began to break out. Rocks were whizzing everywhere as the crowd erupted. The band stopped playing, and while everyone was evacuating the stage the promoter grabbed the mike and said, "Peace, brothers! Love! Let's have peace!" And then, bap!—a rock hit him on the head and knocked him cold.

We started running for our bus. People were screaming and trying to escape while rocks were flying all around us. Dan Wright, our organist, began to run backwards so he could see what was going on behind us. Without any warning, he rammed his back and legs full speed into a tall cactus. We made it to the bus and picked needles out of Dan while we drove all the way back, broke and dejected, to Topeka. A series of disheartening experiences like this led to the decline of our band. We tried so hard to become successful, but nothing good seemed to happen to us.

Our only claim to fame was our experience in New Orleans. We were booked at The Warehouse and given the opportunity to play on the same show with Jim Morrison and The Doors. Kansas opened the show for The Doors on what I believe was the last live performance they ever gave. We were so nervous that we didn't play well that night. Everything seemed to go out of tune, but it was still a great experience. When The Doors finally came on, they had several members of our band come on stage and jam with them on "Light My Fire." We got to talk with Jim Morrison, and found that he had a lot of personal charisma. Shortly after that, Morrison died in France.

On our drive back from New Orleans, our bus threw a rod. This breakdown became symbolic of the breakup of the band. We got into some really desperate financial circumstances, and this opened up a mire of contentions and divisions from which the first Kansas band never recovered. We were headed in different directions musically. Dave and Phil were with one faction that wanted to play more conventional hard-rock music. I, on the other hand, was getting deeper into the development of unorthodox, orchestral jazz-rock-classical music, if you will. It was a very strange marriage of influences, and I suppose I was getting a little too mystical for some of the others. They just wanted to do something a little different, not radically different. So the one-year-old group simply broke up.

We had a meeting about who got possession of the name, but we had already done something a little devious on our side of the fence—we had trademarked it. Thus, the name could only be used by the four of us who had chosen to stay together. The second Kansas band was started by me, Don Montre (the former keyboard player, saxophonist and flutist), Lynn Meredith (the former lead singer), and Dan Wright (the other keyboard player). To complete the band, we needed to find a drummer and a bass player. Zeke Low, the original drummer for Saratoga, became the drummer for Kansas II. For our bass player, we decided on a musician from Lawrence, Kansas named Rod Mikinski. We also added another saxophone player because I had come to like that instrument very much, and it had become an integral part of the type of music I was writing. So we hired John Bolton, a saxophonist and flutist from Manhattan, Kansas, Lynn Meredith's home town.

Musically Kansas II was really a continuation of Kansas I. The musical style did not change appreciably, and neither did our economic circumstances. The others who decided to reform White Clover had a better financial time of it than we had. We continued to be as unconventional and blatantly original as we could possibly be.

This was a very prolific time for me; I seemed to crank out songs nonstop. Some of them fell by the wayside and were never performed. Others were performed for a while and then dropped because I wrote at such a fast pace that we simply couldn't perform them all. The music and lyrics for many of these songs have survived; they weren't always very good, but I would have to say that they were different.

It was during this period that I was beginning to seriously get into various forms of mysticism and Eastern philosophies like Zen. These influences became increasingly apparent in my songs; the music and lyrics were growing more mystical and ethereal.

(I am amused by the September 16, 1971 entry into my diary: "Two days left to be twenty-one. It's sort of depressing to think about. Lives are *really* short.")

The second Kansas band managed to stay fairly busy, and we were able to earn a living with our music. But we seemed to be making little progress, and success kept eluding us. On a couple of occasions, representatives of small record companies came to hear us and expressed some interest in signing the group for a recording contract. These incidents were great sources of hope for us; they became the cohesive force that bound us together.

We all had high aspirations, but nothing much came out of them. There were no contracts, and we were being stifled by insufficient interest in the Midwest in our kind of original music. It appeared to be a classic case of being in the wrong place at the wrong time. I was becoming ambivalent, desperately trying to hold the band together because it was the only thing to hang on to, but at the same time growing increasingly dissatisfied with the band. Just when this dissatisfaction reached a climax after a couple of fresh disappointments for Kansas, something happened that permanently changed the shape of my career.

In 1973, Phil Ehart came to me and told me out of the clear blue, "Let's go out and mess around, talk, whatever." What he really had in mind was an offer to come back to the White Clover group. They felt the need for another writer, and they also wanted a second guitar player. This was one of the most difficult decisions I ever had to make. I had been with the second Kansas band from 1971 to early 1973, and though the breakup of that band appeared inevitable I didn't want to be the one to bring it about. It would mean that I would have to sever or at least injure some close friendships. Don and Dan were two of the best friends I ever had, and all of us had been through a lot together. But something compelled me to pay the price and go back with Dave and Phil.

I joined White Clover, and the members of the second Kansas band decided to go their separate ways. This was unfortunate, because a lot of gifted and talented musicians discontinued their careers in music when that band broke up. White Clover's lead singer was Steve Walsh, and he had a better voice than any I had previously worked with. This was also the first time I had ever worked with another writer who was capable of coming up with creditable material. All in all, we thought we were getting into an artistically healthy situation. The new band also included Rich Williams playing guitar and

violinist Robby Steinhardt. This added a new quality and potential to our music.

I brought a few of the old Kansas songs with me and
immediately plunged into writing new songs for White Clover
so that we would have a broad enough repertoire. We practiced
and learned these songs, but I wondered if our circumstances
would ever improve. It's difficult to say whether the modified
White Clover band was better than the second Kansas band, but
we were certainly more tenacious. There was a lot more drive,
enthusiasm and determination in this group, and this was just
what I needed after lagging through two years of back-to-back
disappointments.

We found ourselves playing the same old local haunts and
driving halfway across the state of Kansas in blizzards and below-
zero weather to play some poorly attended little club for $150.
We did this week after week, clinging firmly to the idea that
someone would rescue us and stick us in a recording studio, and
that it would be all roses after that. And in truth, that's very
nearly what happened.

We were discovered by a man named Wally Gold. A demo
tape that the band made just before I joined had somehow
found its way into the hands of Don Kirshner. Although Don
was a key person in the record and publishing business, we had
never heard of him. He liked what he heard and sent an envoy
out to the obscure little town of Ellinwood, Kansas to hear our
group. By this time, we were in the process of changing our
name. We thought that if we were on the brink of discovery, it
would be unwise to use the name White Clover, a relic of the
dying psychedelic era. Our group really needed a more appropriate name. The second Kansas band had dispersed, and most
of its members stopped pursuing their musical careers. The
name was available, so we became the third Kansas band.

When we heard that an agent from a major recording
company was about to come, we took steps to prepare for this
crucial occasion. We publicized that there would be free beer for
all who would come to hear us in Ellinwood. Kansas brought
several kegs of beer to The Opera House, the little club we were
playing, and the place was stuffed with farmers and kids from

miles around. When Wally Gold arrived to check us out, he thought we were the most popular thing in the five-state area. He didn't realize the place was packed because of the free beer.

Our show probably would have been well attended without the added incentive, because we were growing in popularity. But we didn't want to take any chances. Wally was favorably impressed with our music and stage performance, and within a very short period of time we received a momentous phone call from Don Kirshner saying he wanted to sign us to a recording contract.

Naturally we were ready to sign anything that came our way just to get out of the rut we were in. All of us were getting burned out by the same old routine of playing the club circuit in the Midwest. We thought we were well on our way to fame and fortune when we signed the recording contract. But months passed and nothing happened. For almost a year we sat around waiting, unable to figure out the cause of the delay. We were back to playing the same old local haunts and dives, and all of us were experiencing an embarrassing problem of credibility. A number of the local kids had heard we had signed a contract with a big company, but there was no Kansas record.

One of the clubs we played during this interim period was in Des Moines, Iowa. We were booked for a week at the time of the Iowa State Fair, and all the motels and hotels in town were filled up. We told the club owner we couldn't find a place to stay, so he arranged for us to stay at the house of the club's huge bouncer.

A strange incident took place on our opening night. The place was absolutely packed, and people were jammed right against the stage. After we started to play, we noticed a lot of commotion in the back, but there was too much smoke in the air to tell what was going on. Just then, a guy jumped up on stage, grabbed a microphone, and said, "All right, everybody out the back door *now!*" As the place began to empty, we heard a girl screaming. We walked over to a small crowd in the middle of the floor and saw broken glass everywhere. A big guy was laying on the floor with blood all over his leather jacket.

We found out that a gang of bikers had come in and

instigated a major brawl in the back of the club. The club's bouncer got in a fight with the head of the bike gang when he tried to break up the fight. Seeing that the biker was ready to kill him, he grabbed a beer bottle and broke it. When the gang leader attacked, the bouncer all but severed his assailant's arm with the broken bottle. An ambulance carried him away to the hospital.

Things finally settled down, and all of us were talking about the unusual evening. Suddenly a drunk staggered in and asked for a drink. The club owner turned him away, but he came back in. The owner made him leave a second time, and the third time he literally kicked him out. After a few minutes, we heard an engine racing and the sound of screeching tires. We looked up and "hit the dirt" just as a car came crashing right through the door of the club. The driver was the drunk who had just been kicked out. He jammed on his brakes, threw it into reverse, and roared away, leaving a gaping hole in the front of the building.

We said, "Let's get *out* of here" and canceled the rest of our engagement. We got in our bus and followed the directions to the bouncer's house (he had left early to get his friends to defend his house, thinking that the bikers might seek revenge). The road led us into some woods, and when we came to a hill we saw something that looked like the proverbial haunted house. There wasn't a light on anywhere, so we checked the directions to make sure it was the right place. We pulled the bus up in the driveway and elected Dave to knock on the door. The door immediately flew open and Dave had a double-barrel shotgun right in front of his face. He yelled, "Don't shoot! It's the band! It's the band!"

The bouncer and his friends were inside armed to the teeth, waiting for the bike gang to retaliate that night. We were petrified as we walked in, and they told us, "You guys better stay upstairs." All six of us crammed into a tiny bedroom. We were laying in our sleeping bags and talking about the situation downstairs. Just as we were dropping off to sleep, a gun started to open fire on the house. When it was over, we nervously looked out the window, but there were no bikers outside. Instead, it was the same crazy guy who had driven through the front of the club. He had apparently followed us to the house, thinking that we were the ones who had thrown him out.

The whole thing was like a corporate bad dream, but the next day we got the news that the arrangements had finally been made for us to fly to New York to record our first album.

THE MUSIC OF KANSAS

Kansas, as our album was called, was recorded too hastily. It was completed in less than a month, and the production quality leaves much to be desired. Although we were tremendously excited about the appearance of our first record, we soon grew dissatisfied with it from a technical point of view. But it was the product of years of struggle, and I was happy with the material.

We had taken a giant leap out of our previous morass, and our initiation into the world of popular recording artists had begun.

Kansas has always sought to be a dynamic act on the concert circuit. After the release of our first album in 1974, we proceeded to tour more extensively and intensively than ever. I think our heavy schedule of touring and traveling was Kansas' means of attaining a higher level of success. A number of groups achieve it through a hit single or an album that climbs very high on the charts. We couldn't follow that route initially, because our music was still a bit "off the wall." It was not your typical top-forty sound. So we gradually built up a kind of cult following through our concert tours and developed our own distinctive audience.

The titles of some of the songs on the *Kansas* album had no particular meaning. This was characteristic of my earlier songs and poems because of my quest for originality (I abandoned this practice after the second Kansas album). I named one of these songs "Belexes," and the lyrics vaguely reflected some of my feelings:

Oh, I cannot tell you to make up your mind
And gather together the best of your kind
The prophets have spoken the words of ill fate
Your childhood has ended you've taken the bait
You've got the power it's there deep inside
Just look around and you'll know what you've tried
So much relies on the course that you take
The fool and the wise man both burn at the stake

Look at the heads buried deep in the sand
Hiding from evil made by their own hand
The prophets have spoken the words of ill fate
Your childhood has ended you've taken the bait
You've got the power it's there deep inside
Just look around and you'll know what you've tried
So much relies on the course that you take
The fool and the wise man both burn at the stake[1]

"The prophets" was an allusion to those people from all traditions who have gained depth of insight into the human condition. Eastern religions continually stress the need for an introspective look to find true spiritual power within.

The last two lines of both stanzas held meaning for me, but I couldn't entirely grasp their implications.

Another song was directly inspired by Hermann Hesse's novel, *Narcissus and Goldmund*. I called it "Journey from Maria-bronn":

Two began together, lived as one
Each one to the other had become
More than a friend, living to meet a common end
They were true, each one knew all is well

Still the elder knew it could not last
Hidden memories from the young one's past
Drew them apart
Both knew that deep within his heart they must part
Each their own separate way

It puzzles me how we can be so close and yet worlds
        apart
Can it be, my memory has torn my life in two
From the very start

I screamed for the devil to let me be
I called to the heavens to set me free
Today I prayed for the answer and not one
Of the gods in the sky would rescue me

Dreams of fortune fill the young one's mind
Learn the worldly ways of hope to find
Love on the way, searching to find the light of day
In his soul he had found his own way

But to each other they will soon return
Destiny fulfilled, their words will burn an eternal flame[2]

The lyrics of this song are essentially a synopsis of Hesse's book
which affirms, in part, that the fates of human relationships are
directed by forces and principles external to those relationships.

"Apercu," a French word that means "insight," is the title
of another song on this first album:

The mist of time is still concealing
The vision that I seek
Those who died have all borne witness
If only they could speak

Now and then we've all been given
A glimpse of bygone days
I'd give all to see it clearly
Not shrouded in the haze
Yet I saw it all inside me, for a moment
Were you with me?
Have we done it all before, is there really so much
        more?

Each man has a memory
Much more than the eye can see
Yet still others linger deep inside you
Haunting thoughts of pain and joy divide you
Look beyond your eyes
At the dark and moody skies
For they're standing in your way
And I feel the light of day

Now the earth gives forth its secrets
Held in mountain sea and plain

They have never been forgotten
Only locked inside my brain
While I slept I had a vision, I remember
You were with me
We have done it all before, in our minds behind the
    door[3]

This song is clearly about reincarnation. At first it raises the question, "Have we done it all before . . .?" After alluding to a hidden memory of past lives and "a vision" that caused a fragment of this memory to surface, the song answers the earlier question in the affirmative: "We have done it all before. . . ."

Another song, "Death of Mother Nature Suite," laments the irreversible effects of man's exploitation of nature. Ignorance, self-delusion and arrogance have blinded us to the disastrous consequences that will soon come upon us due to our greedy abuse of natural resources.

While we were touring with our *Kansas* album, my relationship with the first girl I ever dated fell apart. I met Kathy Stout back in 1970 after leaving Washburn University. Our lead singer Lynn Meredith was the matchmaker, and he set me up with Kathy while we were doing a gig in Manhattan, Kansas. It was kind of strange, but she liked me because I was afraid of a spider that lowered itself in front of me while I was performing on stage. We dated for four years and even talked of marriage. But then she dumped me! I couldn't understand it—up until then she had displayed such good taste in men. . . .

In September 1974, while Kathy and I were breaking up, the Kansas band was playing small engagements on a club tour. We went to Atlanta to play at Alex Cooley's Electric Ballroom (now the Agora Ballroom). A girl who knew some of the members of Fresh Start, the opening act, was backstage. We played some eye games, but nothing came out of it—I was too shy.

A few months later (November), we were back at Alex Cooley's for a couple of weeks. One night after we finished our set, I walked by a table and the same girl I had seen backstage in September looked at me and said, "Will you marry me?" I answered, "Let me put my guitar away, and we'll talk about it."

Her name was Vicci, and it turned out that she was using a variation of a line I had used the week before. Upon seeing one of her girlfriends, I had exclaimed, "Whoa—why don't you marry me?" (My shyness was cured by dating several girls after breaking up with Kathy.)

Vicci and I soon fell in love, and over the next several months I flew to Atlanta to see her whenever I could find a break in our almost continual touring schedule. During our times together, Vicci "acculturated" me by bringing me to plays, films, good restaurants, and arts festivals.

On one of these visits (September 1975), I was shocked to find that Vicci had her things packed up. She told me she was ready to move to Topeka so we could be together more often. At that point I realized there would be no sense in our having two apartments, so we decided to get married. I later concluded that she kind of "tricked" me into marriage (I'm glad she did)—I don't think she really intended to move to Topeka!

We were married on December 27, 1975 in Daytona Beach, Florida. Christmas was the only time I was able to get enough time off the tour to get married. After our honeymoon at Disney World, we moved into an apartment in Atlanta (the Kansas band decided to move there because it was so much easier to fly in and out of Atlanta). We bought our first house in March 1977 and moved into our present house in March 1979.

In 1975, we recorded our second album, *Song for America,* in California. The record company was looking for something with more commercial appeal and thought it would not be in our best interest to produce an album like that. But I still happen to like that record very much, because I think that in some ways it was our most creative effort. The songs were generally very long and complex, and they were richly orchestrated. This kind of music further deepened the relationship we had with our cult following, but it did very little to bring our music to a wider audience, and this was of course what the record company wanted.

Our artistic ideals were high, and none of us wanted to give in to any pressure to make our music conform to a different set of standards. Over and over we were told that we should shorten our songs and see if we could put more popular appeal into our music. But we were trying to resist the temptation to commercialize our sound. Instead, we continued to tour and amass a larger following, and this was to become the basis for the success that we later experienced. We just snowballed our way around the country, opening for a lot of prominent groups and taking pride much of the time in blowing them off the stage and stealing the show. Kansas began to get a reputation as an opening act that should be avoided by a lot of the groups. The stronger bands didn't mind playing after us, but other popular groups that were weaker in sound found themselves very much dwarfed by the sound of Kansas. (Here is a partial list of the groups we appeared with: Queen, Jefferson Starship, Leon Russell, Yes, Mott the Hoople, Robin Trower, Hawkwind, Climax Blues Band, R.E.O., Hot Tuna, Fairport Convention, Mahogany Rush, Flock, Guess Who, Ted Nugent, ZZ Top, Outlaws, Bachman Turner Overdrive, Billy Joel, The Kinks, Argent, Blue Oyster Cult, Lynrd Skynrd, Status Quo, Eureka, Canned Heat, Artful Dodger, The Eagles, The Beach Boys, Trapeze, Mike Quatro, Dr. Hook, Edgar Winter, Johnny Winter, Poco, Manfred Mann, Sweet, Rory Gallagher, Bad Co., Bloodrock, Whiz Kids, Peter Frampton, Marshall Tucker, Loggins and Messina, Fleetwood Mac, Bob Seger, Kiss, J. J. Walker, Black Sabbath, Joe Walsh, Elvin Bishop, Wishbone Ash, Masters of the Airwaves, Three Dog Night, Doobie Bros., Chicago, UFO, Fresh Start, Spirit, J. Geils, Rush, Rhythm Aces, Hydra, Journey, Aerosmith, Styx, Foghat, Bonaroo, Dave Mason, Ace, James Montgomery, Harvey Mandel, Herbie Hancock, Luther Allison, Captain Beefheart, Black Oak Arkansas, Head East, and Jo Jo Gunne.)

As this was happening, I found that all of us were getting increasingly engulfed in the whole process of becoming a major rock band. It was a very exciting life-style, and a lot of strange and funny things began to happen as we traveled all over the country. (Diary entry from May 11, 1975: "The gigs at the [Alex Cooley's Electric] Ballroom were great. I always love that place. Friday night was funny. Someone sent champagne up to our dressing room, and everyone was a little loose. As usual, I got talked into doing something ridiculous. The guys scraped together $40 if I would go onstage in my underwear, a clown mask, and black boots. Under the circumstances I agreed. It was one of the strangest sets we ever played, and I was forty bucks richer at the expense of one evening's dignity.")

My intense search for meaning and truth was temporarily taking a back seat to this new way of living. But this does not mean that I completely abandoned my spiritual quest. In fact, I discovered that the Eastern philosophies I was exploring were quite popular among the musicians we were getting to know and often appeared in one form or another in their music. Portions of two other diary entries illustrate the direction my thinking was taking during this time:

> I've been undergoing some internal changes lately, or rather I should say I've reached the next stage of my continually evolving personality. I guess I don't really know myself as well as I thought I did. It's difficult for me to assess my own feelings, and I do and think things that I can't account for. At the same time, I am objectively aware of these things I think and do. I continually observe my own thoughts and actions from a vantage point which is immune to them. In that way I can inwardly laugh at myself when I become angry, sad, inconsiderate of others, or some equally undesirable action. If I can develop this ability, this inner awareness, it will diminish the occurrence of those undesirable thoughts and actions.

> The fact is, I'm prone to nostalgic melancholia. I look back on what I know were bad times and now they seem good. Not that I am in any way dissatisfied with the present, I just have this inherent fascination for things past. Even the fact that the moment in which I wrote the preceding page is gone forever just knocks me out.
> Some Eastern philosophies (and others, for that matter) teach that all exists in the Here and Now, and that all moments exist simultaneously. *That* state of mind is what I seek; to be one with all states of consciousness at every moment.

One of the pieces on the *Song for America* album was called "Incomudro." I saw this word in a dream and used it as a song title to add to the originality. Naturally, I didn't have the faintest idea of what it meant, but it seemed somehow appropriate in connection with the subtitle for this song, "Hymn to the Atman." Atman is the Hindu term for the individual soul, while brahman is used of the universal soul.

INCOMUDRO—HYMN TO THE ATMAN

Run a silent path to nowhere, everything is all
You could have a pleasant life if Summer had no Fall
Treat yourself so gently though the task is often hard
Man is not a God it seems, who holds the final card
Close your eyes and feel the darkness, speak and hear
    the sound,
We only catch a glimpse of all the life that is around,
The man is not alive who knows the value of his soul,
And when our lives are pulled away, there's more to fill
    the hole
I wonder what you'd think if all the changes didn't
    come,
For growing old is only going back to where you're
    from
Far beyond our senseless thought there lies a core of
    gold
Where essence of the newborn child is waiting in the
    old,
The Master Plan is well conceived, it's there for all to
    see
And each day that is spent in thought, is living harmony
Reach into the depths of being, pass beyond the years,
Time is lost in stillness, where there are no hopes and
    fears,
Linger in the void, and like a beacon in the night
Purity will fill your soul with ever-present light
Everything you seek is waiting patiently within
For growing old is only going back to where you've
    been[4]

This song illustrates the syncretistic approach I took to religion as it seeks to combine elements of Hinduism with those of Zen Buddhism. "The man is not alive who knows the value of his soul"—this is the atman, valuable because it can be merged, according to Eastern thought, with the universal soul, the all-that-is.

The concept of reincarnation is most obvious in the line, "For growing old is only going back to where you're from." Zen thought stresses our need to "pass beyond the years" and break away from the bounds of time, space and desire ("Time is lost in stillness, where there are no hopes and fears"). The "void" is a reference to satori or nirvana, the same nothingness sought in all Eastern religions. It can only be achieved by inward illumination—"Everything you seek is waiting patiently within."

"Lamplight Symphony" develops an entirely different kind of experience:

On a winter's night, stars are cold and bright in the sky,
The slumber of the earth is pure and deep
From a distant wood, drifts the echo of a beast
The old man stirs and wakens in the night
He stands before his window gazing at the grave
Forgotten dreams are flashing through his weary mind
And though his life is empty, he pretends that she's still
    there
With hunger in his soul, he yearns for life and love gone
    by,
With memories his one and only joy
All he has to give, he would give to bring back the life,
And raise the one who lies beneath the snow
He lights a lamp and looks at pictures of the past,
The faces of their youth still glow with new-found love,
But the picture's faded, and time has stolen youth away
With a spoken word that he thought he heard from her
    lips,
He felt another presence in the room,
He was filled with fear but filled with joy he arose
And turned to face the image that he knew
She stood before him and her hand reached out for his
A peaceful light shone in her eyes
She said she'd come to soothe him, and someday they'd
    be as one
She began to fade and her image disappeared,

So he was left alone to face the night,
Never in his life, had he been so held in awe,
As he faced the apparition of his wife
He stood before the window gazing at the grave,
And with a lightened heart he saw the first of dawn,
He knew that she was waiting, that someday they'd be
    as one[5]

I had been reading a book about an English woman who claimed to be in contact with the spirits of a number of great composers, including Chopin and Brahms. Through a process of automatic writing, she said that these composers were producing new works through her. The piano compositions that resulted resembled the styles of these musicians, and this naturally led to controversy and speculation.

Intrigued by the idea of spiritistic visitation, I decided to create a musical "ghost story." In this story, an elderly widower is portrayed as looking through the window of his snowy cabin in some remote area. The ghost of his recently departed wife appears and tells him that someday they will be together again.

Masque (1975) was our third album, and it was the product of some troubled times. The pressure that the record company was exerting upon us to commercialize our style reached a peak while we were working on the music for this album. It caused a great deal of tension, because we were beginning to think we were jeopardizing our careers by sticking to our principles of artistic freedom. We didn't want anyone or anything to stifle the length, style or lyrical content of our songs. But simultaneously a seed had been planted in us, and it grew into a craving for material success on a large scale. Thus, we were actually at odds with ourselves.

The pressure of this period is reflected in this diary insert I wrote when we were playing in Seattle, Washington:

> Something different to worry about today. Slowly but surely the world is letting the air out of my musical balloon. I don't have the heart any more to fight tooth and nail just to write and play the music I like. It's just like somebody pulled the plug out of my inspiration. If I write

music that is fresh and creative, people don't want to hear it. But it's totally adverse to my nature to play the same old rehashed crap that people seem to have an inexhaustible appetite for. I just can't do it. We got in another big argument about it last night. Because we didn't play rock and roll, we didn't get as big a reception as the other two bands. I would prefer to play our music no matter what people do, and the rest of the band would rather conform to the situation and play music that they would jump around to. I'm so disappointed at that attitude. Every great composer I've ever looked up to has always refused to let the ways of the world dictate what their art would be. If they had, they would have given up the very energy that made them great. If artists were subject to the wishes of the masses who really don't understand art, then it would cease to exist as a meaningful mode of expression. It would all develop a drab and empty sameness. It's the *deviant* that gives meaning to the whole, and if he is removed, there is nothing but stagnancy. Constant innovation and a spirit of creativity are the only things really worthy of attention.

I have this recurring daydream where I live on a virgin planet in a giant structure which is self-sufficient and contains all that is necessary to create and record great works of music. Nobody to hear it but me and God and my wife. Where would we be without our dreams?

This tension between artistic integrity and commercial success reached a critical level, and something had to give. *Masque* marked a turning point in this respect, because we tried to compromise these antithetical pulls in this album. We wanted to be a very big group, and we were ready to make some limited changes to achieve this goal.

Masque was only slightly more successful than *Song for America,* but it was one step closer. Each new album sold more than the one before, and this was largely due to our relentless touring and stylistic modifications. We managed to play in nearly every state of the union.

The record sleeve of this album defined "masque" as "A disguise of reality created through a theatrical or musical performance." For the cover we chose *Water,* one of the marvelous "composite head" paintings by the sixteenth-century Italian

painter Arcimboldo. This very capable and original artist created the illusion of a portrait by crowding a wide variety of
related objects into a weird composite image. These bizarre
heads could be interpreted either as demons or masks, "depending on whether the observer chooses to emphasize their philosophical (I could say metaphysical) or playful disposition."[6] The
black background of the cover was appropriate to the mood of
the lyrics of the songs I wrote for this album. They dwell on
death, nightmares, and my inability to find meaningful answers
to the dilemmas of life.

"Two Cents Worth" certainly fits in with this dark theme.
In it, I offered my opinion or "two cents worth" about the state
of the world as I saw it then. I felt as though I had been born
in the wrong century; the twentieth-century scene seemed so
corrupt and insane that I could find little room for any kind of
hope.

Well I been drinkin' again
And I know it's a sin
But I just can't refuse an old friend
Cause Life is gettin' me down
And I been two times around
And there ain't nothing but pain around the bend
I'm not made for the time
I'm born in the wrong century
There's too much craziness here
In twenty-five years I have used all the tears in my eyes

Now this old world is a fright
You know my future ain't bright
And I'd just crawl in a hole if I could
Or maybe live out in space
Or some other far away place
And not come back to this earth till it's good
Oh but I'm dreaming again
I know that I'm here till the end
There's too much craziness here
In twenty-five years I have used all the tears in my eyes

Well you might think that I'm all wrong
The things I say in this song
I really wish I could see it your way
Cause there's a storm rollin' in
And it just might be the end
So I'm praying we'll all get away
Now my cup is running dry
The weight of the world gets me down
There's too much craziness here
In twenty-five years I have used all the tears in my eyes

There's nowhere to turn
So I'll just have to learn not to cry, no more
It's all I can do till we find something new
But I'll get by you know I'll try
In twenty-five years I have used all the tears in my eyes[7]

There seemed to be no exit, no way of escape. I knew that if we are left to our own resources, there can be no ultimate basis for meaning and purpose in our existence. The perversity of human nature kept getting me down, and I longed for somewhere to turn for real answers.

Continuing this theme, "Child of Innocence" was written about the inescapable reality of death. The child of innocence is the person who views his life as though death will never strike him; he fails to grasp the reality of his temporal nature. He deludes himself by thinking that death is something that only happens to others:

Sweet child of innocence
Living in the present tense
Father Time will take his toll
Rack your body and steal your soul
What became of all the years
Are you drowning in your tears
Who will catch you when you fall
Who will hear you when you call

(Chorus)

I will comfort you, take your hand and see you through
I will take you through the door

Who do you think you are
Try to live forever and you won't get far
I wait behind your door
Makes no difference if you're rich or poor
Though you're weary and afraid
Still you try to flee my blade
Come and walk in my new land
If you'll only take my hand

In the image of those that have walked before me here
I am cast in the web of an ancient spell
I am holding on to life, I'm drifting in the stream
Everything's much clearer now
We live within a dream and never wake

Judge not by what you see
More than you can count are here with me
Give up your foolish pride
All that walk the earth have died![8]

The angel of death sings this song to the child of innocence, and this is especially obvious in the chorus. The "blade"
specifically refers to the image of the grim reaper. I often found
myself dwelling on this negative and ominous theme, well-sum-
marized in the last verse. The truth of this song was undeniable,
but again I had nowhere to turn.

The last two songs on the *Masque* album can be regarded
as two sides of the same coin. "Mysteries and Mayhem" is full
of obscure lyrics because it was an attempt to describe an arcane
nightmare.

Well I'm trying to tell you about a thing I thought I saw
It came to me in a dream one night
When a voice began to call
I heard my name being summoned as I looked around
    to see
A hooded judge and jury
There was no mercy there for me
Well I can't make it, I just can't figure it out
This dream is drivin' me crazy
I gotta know what it's all about
The Mark is upon me, and the Mark of Cain brings fear

A cold wind's blowin' right down my back
I'm runnin', I'm runnin' from a figure that's dressed in
     black
I think my legs are made out of lead
Cause I'm runnin' but I'm going nowhere
The bad dream is coming closer and closer
I got a feelin' he'll always be there
Forever is a long time to spend in agony
And the demons of confusion have got a place for me
The Mark is upon me

I was tired, so tired of runnin'
I had to turn and look around
I saw eyes that looked right through me
And a voice that made no sound
My body froze and I stood and stared, unearthly face
before me, From the depths of a hooded Nightmare
I saw what could not be
Mysteries and mayhem from the pinnacle I see
There's no answer when there's no question
The Mark of Cain bears hard on me[9]

The words are unclear because it is extremely difficult to
communicate the reality of a nightmare to someone else. The
song as a whole does not have a particular message apart from
the idea of a relentless pursuit. I didn't know the significance of
the "Mark of Cain," but the words rang in my ears. The penulti-
mate line ("There's no answer when there's no question") is an
allusion to the *koans* of Zen Buddhism. A Zen *koan* is a paradoxi-
cal question that has no rational answer.

Some of the most interesting lyrics that ever came out of
me are in "The Pinnacle," a song that described my attempt to
grasp at what I thought was unattainable.

I've so much to say, and yet I cannot speak
Come and do my bidding now for I have grown too
     weak
My weary eyes have seen all that life can give
Come to me, O young one, for you I can forgive

I stood where no man goes, and conquered demon foes
With Glory and Passion no longer in fashion
The Hero breaks his blade

Cast the Shadow long that I may hide my face
And in this cloak of darkness the world I will embrace
In all that I endure, of one thing I am sure
Knowledge and Reason change like the Season
A Jester's Promenade

Lying at my feet I see the offering you bring
The Mark of Cain is on our faces, borne of suffering
O, I long to see you say it's not been wrong
I stand before you now, a riddle in my song
The answer is that sweet refrain
Unheard it always will remain
Beyond our reach, beyond our gain

Trapped in Life's Parade, a king without a crown,
In this joy of madness, my smile might seem a frown
With talons wrought of steel, I tore the heart of doom
And in one gleaming moment I saw beyond the tomb
I stood where no man goes, above the din I rose
Life is amusing though we are losing
Drowned in tears of awe[10]

I found that I was moving from one philosophy to another,
but nothing could rid me of the emptiness I felt or provide real
meaning and satisfaction. "Knowledge and Reason change like
the Season/A Jester's Promenade." The promenade of human
philosophies and religions was beginning to look like a huge,
insipid joke. My only consolation was in my worship of music
("The answer is that sweet refrain").

A year later (1976), our contractual obligation called for us
to record another album. For some reason, Steve was temporarily dried up as a writer; so the burden fell on me to write most
of the material for the album we called *Leftoverture*. This album
was different from *Masque* in that it was far more commercially
oriented. But this was not as a result of the pressure that was
upon us. We simply decided to ignore all the pressure, because
it had been such a source of tension when we were recording
Masque. Instead, we resolved to move in our own musical direction. Oddly enough, when we did this some of the commercial
element the company had been trying to inject into our music
just naturally surfaced of its own accord.

This was most evident in the first song, "Carry On Wayward Son." The tune was so catchy that this song became our first bona fide hit. The single was very big, and the album went gold, then platinum, then double platinum, and then triple platinum (three million records). The most exciting thing I remember happening to us was when *Leftoverture* became our first gold album; it created quite a sense of accomplishment. We had gone from playing small clubs in rural Kansas for years, barely subsisting on a diet of rice and beans, all the way to recording a gold album, putting us in the upper echelon of recording artists. Now after selling over ten million albums, we have gold and platinum records hanging all over the walls; but the first one was the most momentous.

"Carry On Wayward Son," the first song in our fourth album, picks up and further develops the theme of "The Pinnacle," the last song in our third album. One of the last lines in "The Pinnacle" reads, "I stood where no man goes, above the din I rose." The same image is repeated in the first line of "Carry On Wayward Son": "Once I rose above the noise and confusion." Both songs are about a quest for something that seemed unattainable, but the second contains more of an element of hope.

CARRY ON WAYWARD SON

Once I rose above the noise and confusion
Just to get a glimpse beyond the illusion
I was soaring ever higher, but I flew too high
Though my eyes could see I still was a blind man
Though my mind could think I still was a mad man
I hear the voices when I'm dreamin' I can hear them
say

Carry on my wayward son,
For there'll be peace when you are done
Lay your weary head to rest
Now don't you cry no more

Masquerading as a man with a reason
My charade is the event of the season
And if I claim to be a wise man, it surely means that I
    don't know
On a stormy sea of moving emotion
Tossed about I'm like a ship on the ocean
I set a course for winds of fortune, but I hear the voices
    say

Carry on, you will always remember
Carry on, nothing equals the splendor
Now your life's no longer empty
Surely heaven waits for you

(Repeat chorus)[11]

My goal was inaccessible, but I felt a profound urge to
"carry on" and continue the search. I saw myself as the "wayward son," alienated from ultimate reality, and yet striving to
know it or him. The positive note at the end ("Now your life's
no longer empty/Surely heaven waits for you") seemed strange
and premature, but I felt impelled to include it in the lyrics. It
proved to be prophetic.

"The Wall" was an accurate and eloquent summary of my
thinking during this time:

I'm woven in a fantasy, I can't believe the things I see
The path that I have chosen now has led me to a wall
And with each passing day I feel a little more like
    something dear was lost
It rises now before me, a dark and silent barrier
    between,
All I am, and all that I would ever want to be
It's just a travesty, towering, marking off the boundaries
    my spirit would erase

To pass beyond is what I seek, I fear that I may be too
    weak
And those are few who've seen it through to glimpse
    the other side,
The promised land is waiting like a maiden that is soon
    to be a bride
The moment is a masterpiece, the weight of indecision's
    in the air

It's standing there, the symbol and the sum of all that's
    me
It's just a travesty, towering, blocking out the light and
    blinding me
I want to see

Gold and diamonds cast a spell, it's not for me I know
    it well
The treasures that I seek are waiting on the other side
There's more than I can measure in the treasure of the
    love that I can find
And though it's always been with me, I must tear down
    the Wall and let it be
All I am, and all that I was ever meant to be, in
    harmony
Shining true and smiling back at all who wait to cross
THERE IS NO LOSS[12]

Looking back, I regard the lyrics to "The Pinnacle" and "The Wall" as the best I have written. Somehow the wall was in me, and I did not have the power to remove this barrier to the depths of joy and harmony I so desperately sought.

This search was also reflected in "Miracles Out of Nowhere":

On a crystal morning I can see the dewdrops falling
Down from a gleaming heaven, I can hear the voices
    call
When you comin' home now, son, the World is not for
    you
Tell me what's your point of view

Hey there Mister Madman, what'cha know that I don't
    know
Tell me some crazy stories, let me know who runs this
    show
Glassy-eyed and laughing, he turns and walks away
Tell me what made you that way

(Chorus)

    Here I am just waiting for a sign
    Asking questions, learning all the time
    It's always here, it's always there
    It's just love, and miracles out of nowhere

Tell me now dear Mother, what's it like to be so old
Children grown and leavin', seems the world is growin'
    cold
And though your body's ailin' you, your mind is just
    like new
Tell me where you're goin' to

    It's so simple right before your eyes
    If you'll look through this disguise
    It's always here, it's always there
    It's just love and miracles out of nowhere

I sang this song a hundred, maybe a thousand years ago
No one ever listens, I just play and then I go
Off into the sunset like the western heroes do
Tell me what you're gonna do

    Here I am, I'm sure to see a sign
    All my life I knew that it was mine
    It's always here, it's always there
    It's just love and miracles out of nowhere[13]

I felt like a sojourner on this planet—"Down from a gleaming heaven, I can hear the voices call/When you comin' home now, son, the World is not for you." The home I sought was elsewhere, but again I did not know where to look. Nevertheless, the last chorus, like the end of "Carry On Wayward Son," has a positive ring to it.

It's interesting to see these songs in retrospect, because things that I only later came to understand sometimes came through in the lyrics. This is the case with some of the lines in "Opus Insert":

There's a reason for all that rhymes,
    it's the fact and the way of the times
It's moving emotion, it's high and it's low,
    no matter where you go
There is something for all who look,
    there's a story in every book
All of the pages, between all the lines,
    so much that you can find

But there's too many empty lives my friend
And we just can't let them waste away
For this life is a precious thing my friend
And we just can't wait another day

There's a message in every word, and it's more than the
  word you heard
It's moving emotion, it comes like a sea, washing all
  over me

For there's nothing that we can't do my friend, cause
  the spirit is with us all
And it's here and it's now, it's up and it's down
You can feel it surrounding us all.

After all we're all the same, only difference is a name
  and where we are
In this crazy mixed up deal, there's so much that you
  can feel
Near and far it's where you are

And there's times when I can't contain all the feelings of
  love I'll gain
It's there for the asking, it's for all of you if you would
  take it too

(Repeat chorus)[14]

The word "spirit" was supposed to have an upper case "S,"
though I wasn't sure what I meant by this concept.

Another song on the *Leftoverture* album was called "Cheyenne Anthem." I was developing a special affinity for the American Indian at this time, and books like *Black Elk Speaks* and *Bury
My Heart at Wounded Knee* deeply impressed my thinking. I wrote
this song partly about the predicament and partly about the
world view of the American Indian, a world view that recog-
nized the transitory nature of all worldly things.

CHEYENNE ANTHEM

From the mountains to the sun, Life has only just begun
We wed this land and pledge our souls to meet its end,

Life has only just begun
Here my people roam the earth, in the kingdom of our
    birth,
Where the dust of all our horses hides the sun
We are mighty on the earth, on the earth

You have come to move me, take me from my ancient
    home,
Land of my fathers I can't leave you now
We will share it with you, no man owns this earth we're
    on
Now the wheels are rolling, hear the howling winds of
    war
It's my destiny to fight and die
Is there no solution, can we find no other way, Lord let
    me stay
Under the endless sky and the earth below
Here I was born to live and I will never go, oh no

But we cannot endure like the earth and the mountains
Life is not ours to keep, for a new sun is rising

Soon these days shall pass away, for our freedom we
    must pay
All our words and deeds are carried on the wind,

In the ground our bodies lay, here we lay[15]

The grim reaper takes away not only the lives of people but also of civilizations.

On our 1976 tour with the music from *Leftoverture,* everything was different—Kansas was no longer an opening act; it was the headlining act. Our first tour as the main attraction was quite triumphant. We had achieved a level of success that far exceeded our expectation or hope, and this generated a brand-new kind of pressure to deal with. How could we continue to live up to what we had accomplished? It was only too obvious to us that few rock groups could rest for long on their past achievements. We didn't want to be another "hit and run" band, racking up one big hit and then fading into an unhappy obscurity.

Our fears were overcome by the overwhelming success of our next album, *Point of Know Return.* "Dust in the Wind" turned out to be a far bigger hit than even "Carry On Wayward Son" had been. The single itself went gold, and the album reached triple platinum. Our 1977 tour was the most successful yet, and Kansas seemed to be riding on the crest of the wave.

"Dust in the Wind" represented a radical departure from the musical style that we had established. It was more of a ballad, and the melody and instrumentation were so alluring that it was commercially viable on every level. Another reason for its appeal was that it struck a deep and plaintive chord within a lot of people.

Oddly enough, I did not originally intend for the group even to play this song. I had actually written it as a finger exercise for acoustic guitar. Vicci heard me playing it in my little music room in our house, and as she walked by she said, "That's very pretty; you should put words to that." When I sat down to do so, the lyrics almost spewed out. I did not consciously plan to write words that would be so very morose or bleak in their outlook. They were more a reflection of my inner despair and longing for something that would not pass away, something eternal. In spite of the popularity and financial success of Kansas, I did not really feel good about these achievements. The thought kept emerging from the back of my mind that all this was going to disappear, and that it had no lasting significance. I was grasping for something deeper, and "Dust in the Wind" was a kind of cry to the world saying, "It doesn't really mean anything if you're rich or poor—there has to be something more than this."

DUST IN THE WIND

I close my eyes, only for a moment and
the moment's gone
All my dreams, pass before my eyes
a curiosity

Dust in the wind, All they are is dust
in the wind

Same old song, just a drop of water
in an endless Sea
All we do, crumbles to the ground
though we refuse to see

Dust in the wind, All we are is dust
in the wind

Don't hang on, nothing lasts forever
but the earth and sky
It slips away, all your money won't
another minute buy

Dust in the wind, All we are is dust
in the wind[16]

These lyrics more explicitly expressed the transitory nature of things than any of my previous songs, and many people were able to identify with them. The phrase, "nothing lasts forever but the earth and sky" was taken directly from the Indian idea that the earth is eternal but man passes away.

Another song on our *Point of Know Return* album was called "Paradox":

I'm on fire
Burning with a question in my mind
Strange desire
Seems there's nothing else for me to find

'Cause I've been here and I've been there
Seems like I've been everywhere before
I've seen it all a hundred times
Still I think there surely must be more

I been livin', I had to take my time and
change my style
Now I wonder, is something going to
make it all worthwhile?

I know there's more than meets the eye
Like to see it 'fore I die for sure
Something tells me it's all right
Only one step farther to the door

There ain't no feelin', feels the same as
findin' out the key

> Now I'm reelin', thinking of the things
> that I might see
>
> I'm not afraid to face the light
> I'm not afraid to think that I might fall
> I was going nowhere fast
> I was needin' something that would last[17]

The message of this song is similar to that of "Dust in the Wind," but it looks at it from a different angle. By this time, I had sampled wares from a whole cafeteria of religious choices, but none of them proved satisfying. Many of them were varia-tions on the same theme (the inner quest), and it was as though I was going in circles. I kept changing directions, but I couldn't find a way out ("I've been here and I've been there/Seems like I've been everywhere before"). And yet I was prodded on by a hope that there had to be some form of ultimate meaning and purpose to our existence ("Still I think there surely must be more"). Something would have to lift me up out of the maze I was in, and more than anything I wanted that to happen ("I know there's more than meets the eye/Like to see it 'fore I die. . . . I'm not afraid to face the light").

Would my search for "something that would last" be mocked by endless silence? If, as Carl Sagan and others claim, the cos-mos is all that was, is, or ever will be, the answer would be yes. But just as surely as food corresponded to my need to eat and other personalities corresponded to my want of companionship and dialogue, I kept believing that something or Someone very real could fulfill my implanted appetite for eternity.

This diary entry from December 5, 1977 ties in closely to the theme of "Paradox":

> I think what I really need is to meet my guru. (If I said that to anyone in the band I would be laughed out of the room.) I don't necessarily mean I need to physically meet someone, I just need to come to a great point of understanding of the nature of my existence. I'm thirsty for wisdom, and peace, and I desperately fear that I'm not making any progress. My increasing wealth has brought me security, but no greater happiness. My fame has only

resulted in a lack of privacy. . . . My life seems to be at odds with what I seek, or think I seek. And deep down inside, I can see clear through these people and events, and feelings, but I just don't know what to make of it. What does it all lead up to? My mind is so clouded by this dilemma that it's so difficult for me to be happy. I can't even fully discern the nature of the dilemma itself. I read all kinds of books about sages and mystics and holy men and I understand it, I really do, but I just can't *feel* it yet. Can enlightenment possibly be *disappointing*?

"Sparks of the Tempest" was written soon after I read George Orwell's *1984*. This is a song about totalitarianism, or "the age of the gun." This book was all the more chilling to me because the technology, the machinery, and the ethos of Western culture made it ominously prophetic. People seem increasingly willing to sacrifice their freedom in exchange for what one perceptive writer calls "personal peace and affluence."[18] "Your future is managed and your freedom's a joke/You don't know the difference as you put on the yoke. . . . Though they may promise, they only bring pain."[19]

The scenario in the next song, "Nobody's Home," involves a visitation from a representative of an extraterrestrial civilization from another part of the galaxy. At this time, I entertained the distant hope that our planet might be rescued by some benevolent alien. But in this song, the timing was just off; the needed visitation was too late. The friendly emissary "came to learn perhaps to teach," but his arrival took place just after a global nuclear holocaust, and earth was devoid of humanity— "Nobody's Home."

A lot of people thought "Portrait (He Knew)" was about Christ, but at the time I wrote this song I wasn't doing a lot of thinking about Christ. Instead, this was a musical portrait of Albert Einstein (though it could also apply to a number of historical figures with an extraordinary measure of charisma and vision). Some of the books I was reading acclaimed the far-reaching contributions Einstein had made to theoretical physics. Our view of the nature of the universe was revolutionized by the creative genius of this man who refused to take things for granted or to be bound by conventional models of reality. And I wondered, Where was he going? What might have happened if he had been given another quarter-century? At the end of his life, he was searching hard to find the missing elements in his unified field theory. Athough Einstein was not theistic in his perspective, he believed that the cosmos was not simply a product of time plus chance. There had to be more.

The last song on the *Point of Know Return* album is called "Hopelessly Human." My attempt to amalgamate a variety of religious views into one somewhat coherent whole comes through fairly clearly in these lyrics:

> It's a strange aberration, this brain-
> storm of youth
> Though it's lost in translation from
> fancy to truth
> It's hopelessly human both inside
> and out
> A joyous occasion, no reason to doubt
> It's easy somehow, what once was
> elusive is calling me now
>
> I am waiting, I am patiently,
> Doing nothing, in a reverie
> Climbing higher, seeing everything
> Interacting, slowly spiraling
> I am giving, while I'm watching the
> Life I'm living, precious energy
> Escalating, what was once just a game
> It's never the same, no one's to blame
>
> It's a strange situation, there's no
> cause for alarm
> All these hot licks and rhetoric
> surely do you no harm
> They're helplessly human, both
> inside and out
> A joyous occasion, there's no reason
> to doubt
> When each word is read, would you
> know the difference
> If nothing was said

All is rhythm, all is unity
I am laughing, as it's meant to be
Just amusing, I am using the
Word was given, making harmony
Moving slowly, dancing aimlessly
Endless circle, turning fearlessly
Resurrected, falling down again
Introspected, I'm just stating
my views
Now you can choose, what do you
feel
Is it for real this time[20]

All the labors, relationships, dreams and fears of humanity, from an Eastern perspective, are a tiny part of the cosmic dance. The material or phenomenal world is a powerful deception (*maya*) that disguises the absolute unity of all things. It is really a cosmic play or game (*lila*) from an absolute standpoint. Each of us has a moral duty (*dharma*) to fulfill, but it is also the *dharma* or principle of the universe to move through an unending cycle of creation, preservation and destruction: "Endless circle, turning fearlessly/Resurrected, falling down again." I was "just stating my views" here, but in my syncretism I kept looking for a way to fuse Eastern and Western thought.

Our 1978 album, *Two for the Show,* was recorded live at various locations during our 1977-78 tours. We wanted these two records to show that Kansas is a viable live act outside of the recording studio.

Monolith appeared in 1979, and one of the songs reflected a desperation I had been going through. For years I had found myself driven by a relentless desire to discover the real basis for meaning and purpose. "On the Other Side" was a song about having nothing more to say about these things. I was compelled to write, and yet I had expressed the same thoughts in previous songs. "The empty page before me now, the pen is in my hand/the words don't come so easy but I'm trying. . . . Though I've said it all before, I'll say it once again (one more time)/everyone needs something to believe in."[21] And yet I knew that somewhere, there had to be a limitless source of inspiration.

Appendix to Chapter 7

Here are a few unpublished song lyrics that I wrote between 1971 and 1976.

SPACE POEM (1971)

In the dark lives the light
In the day lives the night

Answers wait for those who seek,
Looking to the skies

Stars above turning slowly
Ancient sun burning holy

Life's begun, born in Heaven
We shall return in the ending
Timeless space lies in waiting
New man born, ever changing

Answers wait for those who seek
Looking to the skies

Worlds are waiting there that eyes have never seen
Time has not been kind, it's not for us to know
We are but dreaming children
Much too young to go

THE SONG WITHIN US (1972)
(SOMBER SYMPHONY)

Black and gloom upon me, in my soul I feel its weight
After years you learn the fears that children never know
In my lonely room, I contemplate my doom
And I know it isn't right

There are some among us, those who feel as much as I
Still they live and love and die and never wonder why
Oh, to be that wise, wearing no disguise
And to feel no pain inside

There's a somber feeling in the air, but here I'll stay
Now the vision's gone, like a ghost it faded away

Once I walked in the light of the morning sun
I felt the glow of a life that had just begun
Now I know that I lost but I'll dream I won
Holy men come and go, and they leave wisdom
Shining, glowing, showing us the way
Here I am feeling sad, when it's so easy
Living is a stage we all go through

There's a song within us, you can hear it if you try
Life can be a fantasy and no one ever dies
You have always been, and will always be
A child forever growing, knowing

A CELEBRATION OF PURE THOUGHT (1972)
(THEOPHANY)

Take a moment to realize what you're doing here
Are you filled with fear by the thought of opening your
    soul?
Do you feel the presence of the other you and the inner
    love?
Let it be the one whose voice you hear

Joy and sorrows, all tomorrow's harmony
Dreams and visions our decisions fill the void

The beginning and the end are both within the thoughts
    you send
Every thing that is was meant to be
You are the one made manifest till all creation's laid to
    rest
We must live according to the plan

Don't refuse, you'll only lose it in the end
Give yourself, fulfill a purpose, grow with time

THEOPHANY II (1973)

Lord, what is this gift you give
It's confusing just to live
Like leaves we wither in the fall
This really can't be all

We are the pattern of the years
And in spite of all your fears the world will keep on
        changing
Why is the question that you cry
When it's time for you to die
Don't you see it's only learning

Then why am I afraid, and when I've found it out
The teachings I have learned, will they erase my doubt?

Hard to believe we meet an end
When we're caught up in the trend
Dream and pretend you'll always be
Till the day you finally see

See, you know that you will find
The answer's in your mind
Tear down the walls that bind you
Journey back to where you've been
The world you're living in is just a passing lesson

But who can I believe when everyone is right
Which one speaks the truth
I'm blinded by the light

UNTITLED (1973)

Now the folly has begun, from our calling we have run
And we look the other way

Time has failed to make us wise, will we never realize
The things that we could do

In His image we were made, and from it we have
        strayed
If only you could see what you are

Let us all regain, the glory not the shame

You and I are both to blame, for fortune and for fame
We'd sell our very souls
Morals have been trod beneath our feet, our justice is
        deceit,
And the dollar is the Lord

Though we revel in our sin, the knowledge deep within
Reminds us all of what we could be

For great men walked the earth, and from their very
    birth
Their destiny was made with deeds that will not fade

Now there's no need to pretend, there's little to defend
Of a race that once was proud
Mothers you better watch your sons for they're the only
    ones
Whose innocence is pure

Let us all regain the glory not the shame
For there's so much to give
And help each other live

CLOSET CHRONICLES (1973)

I'm carried in the current, I'm being swept away
The king is in the closet, he's hiding from the day
I'm caught with a monkey on my back, he's laughing all
    the way
But you don't even hear the words I say
You tell me I'm not living according to the plan
I think I'd rather be a dog more noble than a man
I'd roam the streets at sundown and bark at all the
    bums
Howling at the moon till morning comes

The good ship Mary never left the bay
The captain's on a bender, sleeping in the hay
Dreaming of a maiden lying at his side
Someday he would have her as his bride
Gazing at a portrait as the paint begins to run
Cries the poor mortician, My work is never done
With fear and loathing in his eyes my monkey jumps
    away
And all the time I'm begging him to stay

The king peeped through the doorway to see what had
    transpired
A thousand shouts of malice declared that he was fired
He took a hatchet in his hand and started for the door

He cried I'll be a prophet for the poor
And from the eyes of a bird above, it all appears so vain
I realized that the bird was me and I could feel no pain
So I tell you now as I fly away, carried on the wind
Take it with a grain of salt my friend

A STONE'S THROW FROM HEAVEN (1974)

Tempests rage at midnight
A new day's born at dawn,
The child is father to the man
Before the man is gone
Time is passing slowly, or maybe not at all,
Who's to say what's in or out, when no one's in at all
There's too much to remember, and too much to
          endure,
Half of life escapes you and the other is not sure
Though you are bewildered,
And lost among the sheep,
Follow in the steps of those whose countenance is deep

A never ending promise,
Is given to each name
We're waiting for the fullness while living in the game
Floating on the River,
Not afraid to drown,
The Lord of all creation is searching for his Crown

Tear down the wall that's surrounding your goal,
Open the gates to the world of the soul
We rise and fall like the tide,
Living a stone's throw from Heaven

UNTITLED (1975)

Endless, it reaches to the stars
Beyond it lies the emptiness of Heaven
Gleaming like diamonds in the sun
It reaches to the hearts of all the living

Nameless, you've known it all your life
It waits in every dream for you to follow
Formless, it's found in every form
The treasure of the ages lies before you

Paradise is just within your reach
All your life's a game that's meant to teach

Ten thousand years have come and gone
And still we have eluded what we came for
Standing in sight of all we seek
We're caught up in the wheel that keeps on turning

A PRIORI VOODOO (1975)

There's a place where we can go
We can leave the world behind
When the gates are open wide
There are treasures we can find

O, joy of the unspoken word
Surely waiting to be heard
It lies in wait for the moment to come

There's a sanctuary here
It was waiting all the time
It was lost behind the wall
In the masquerade and mime

O, joy of the unbroken man
He is gentle as a lamb
He stands in the midst of a tempest of woe

A kaleidoscope of thought
Paints the picture that we see
We are swirling in the dance
Of the ghosts that wish to be

We run from the truth yet we feel
For the things we know are real
We search on the outside for that which is in

A KNIGHT IN RUSTY ARMOR (1975)

The Knight in rusty armor goes to war,
And once again the world is calling for a Hero
One to bear the pain
In some lonely foreign land he'll make his futile stand
For causes long forgotten

WAR TOY (1976)

A children's tale is told, of soldiers brave and bold
they learn of war and death, each day from their first
      breath

With guns and knives they kill, although they're children
      still
pretending to be old, their fragile minds unfold

(Chorus)

War toy, war toy, our children learn your ways
War toy

A part of every boy, you seem their source of joy
A harmless fantasy, you're what they want to be

URANTIA

My desire to find religious truth throughout these years with the three Kansas bands was actually accentuated by our attainment of success. Our biggest hit, "Dust in the Wind," was a pensive meditation on the brevity of life; nothing seemed to be immune to the ravages of time. But this song was not written out of sour grapes; I wrote it at a high point in our careers. I didn't know what I was looking for yet, but I knew it was something deeper than material success.

The search continued, but I was becoming disenchanted with Eastern philosophy. A very basic element that needed fulfillment within me seemed to be minimized in these systems. That was a sense of righteousness—an absolute basis for right and wrong. Eastern teachings so stressed the unity of all things that they reduced good and evil to two sides of the same coin. Even Krishna's manifestation of himself to Arjuna in the *Bhagavad Gita* in his universal form illustrates this problem. As the One who manifests the Many, Krishna displays and absorbs all things, both the divine and the demonic.[1]

Eastern religions have a very high reverence for life; but with an ultimate reality that is impersonal (Brahman or the Tao, for instance), they lack a final ground for personal righteousness. I knew that this was a moral universe and that morality only has meaning in the context of personhood—intelligence and choice. Deep inside I was looking for the infinite Person who alone could account for order, aesthetics, intelligence, morality and human life.

But at this time, the only thing I could really cling to was the tremendous emotional experience that resulted from creating and performing music. So I began to worship music more than ever; in a real sense, it became my god. I worshiped it because it was the one thing that made me jubilant and gave me a feeling that I was expressing something that carried weight. Through the medium of music, I sought after truth and tried to strike a common chord with others who were doing the same. The process of writing music was sometimes like a mystical experience; when I gave myself over to it sounds and words would come out, but they seemed disconnected from me as though they were coming from another source.

It only took a little reflection, however, to realize that music could not be the final purpose to my existence. In my more honest moments I realized that it was only a surrogate god, a meager stand-in for something I could not name.

Another thing that ate away at me was the effect our music was having on a large number of people. During each Kansas tour, I would stand on the stage night after night and look out over a sea of thousands of faces. Many were faces of adulation and even adoration directed at us and our music. This near-worship began to make me extremely uncomfortable. I knew what an utterly unworthy object of worship we were, and it distressed me that the same thing was happening with the devotees of many other rock bands as well.

Knowing that my lyrics were having a profound effect on many lives, I felt compelled to accelerate my search to find the truth. The enormous amount of fan mail and the thousands of questions people were asking because of the mystical and transcendental themes in my songs gave me a growing sense of responsibility. These people thought I was some kind of a prophet and that I knew something they didn't know. Many began to look up to me as a musical guru who had the power to send them messages from the cosmic beyond. This began to weigh heavily upon my shoulders. People were looking to me for answers, and I didn't know what the answers were. I felt like a sham and hungered more than ever to discover the true God.

Because of my church upbringing, I assumed that I had

Kerry with the Hotshots, 1954

With my Sears guitar, 1966

The Gimlets in my living room, 1967
From left: Dan Wright, Tim Strauss, me,
Scott Kessler, Carl Corona

The only known photograph of Kansas I, 1970
From left: Phil Ehart, Lynn Meredith, Dave Hope, me, Dan Wright, Larry Baker, Greg Allen, Don Montre

Kansas II, 1971
From left: Don Montre, Dan Wright,
Zeke Low, Rod Mikinski, Lynn Meredith, John Bolton, me

In Lawrence, Kansas with Kansas II, 1972

Kansas III, 1974
From left: Dave Hope, Rich Williams,
Robby Steinhardt (front),
Phil Ehart (back), Steve Walsh, me

Point of know return tour, 1977

Kerry and Vicci at our first
platinum party in New York, 1977

Robby and I, 1978

Kansas with John Elefante, 1982
From left: Dave Hope, me, Rich Williams,
Phil Ehart, Robby Steinhardt, John Elefante

At home, 1982

already tried Christianity and found it wanting. I had long since shoved the Christian message into the back of my mind along with a lot of other childhood memories and had no intention of retrieving it for serious reconsideration. I didn't know it at the time, but I had been inoculated with just enough Christianity to become immune to the real thing.

As a result of the Jesus movement of the late sixties and early seventies, I had come to stereotype Christians as falling into one of two extremes. A Christian was either a hypocrite who went to church on Sundays as a social maneuver, or a wild-eyed Jesus freak who fanatically threw tracts at people on the street and told them they were going to fry in hell. With impressions like these, it is little wonder that I eliminated Christianity as a viable option in my consideration of world views. I had not yet met anyone who could offer an intelligent defense of the Christian perspective.

By 1976 I had backed away from my enthrallment with Eastern philosophies and mellowed into a position that found bits of truth in the doctrines of all religions. I did not want to be exclusivistic, but it grew increasingly clear to me that I still had not found the clear revelation of God that I was desperately searching for all these years. I wanted a focal point or a framework that would draw all truth together under one roof and make coherent sense out of everything I had learned. Was there anything that was broad enough to encompass the truths of all religions?

Then it happened—in 1977 I discovered a book that convinced me I had reached the end of my quest. Actually, I had seen this book before. Whenever I went to a bookstore, I would browse through the religion and occult sections to spot anything that might offer me new perspectives. Sitting way up on the top shelf of the occult section of the Ansley Mall Bookstore in Atlanta was a very large and inviting book. Intrigued by its size, I decided to reach up and look it over. It was called *The Urantia Book*. I thumbed through its 2,097 pages rather briefly and noticed a number of bizarre headings, such as The Seven Super-universes, The Supreme Trinity Personalities, The Local Universe Mother Spirit, and The History of Urantia (our planet).

Some of these things were attractive, but the whole thing sounded a little too far out. I put it back on the shelf and promptly forgot about it.

About a year later (1977) we were in the recording studio in Atlanta, and our engineer Brad Aaron asked me if I had ever read *The Urantia Book.* I replied "Well, no, I remember seeing it once. Why do you ask?" He said that after studying my lyrics, he thought it was something I would really be interested in. Brad's examination of my songs convinced him that this would be the next thing in my path. I told him that it looked intriguing once and promised that I'd look it up, even though it sounded a bit weird. So I went back to the same bookstore (I had never seen it anywhere else), reached up to the same top shelf, and bought the book that seemed to have been patiently waiting for my return.

After shelling out about thirty dollars for *The Urantia Book,* I brought it home and began to examine it as I sat in bed. This time it looked more appealing than it did the first time I browsed through it. In fact, it soon became totally engrossing. I started to delve into it very deeply, and the more I read, the more amazing it became.

The book seemed to be so phenomenal that I stayed up until about 4:30 A.M. reading and experiencing what I thought was the ultimate revelation. All this time I kept waking Vicci up, saying, "Vicci, listen to this!" This book appeared to have all the answers I had been looking for. Later that morning I suddenly awoke out of a sound sleep literally shaking with excitement. I had to share it with someone, and poor Vicci of course thought I was just going through another one of my religious phases. But as I continued to pore over *The Urantia Book* in the ensuing days and months, my initial fascination increased almost to an obsession.

I was resolutely convinced that I had discovered the supreme revelation I had been looking for. There were a number of reasons for this conviction. First, this book was more diverse than any book I had ever read. It was written by numerous authors and contained a wealth of amazing information about God, the universe and man. It was also surrounded by an aura of mystery, because the authors (e.g., Divine Counselor, Perfector of Wisdom, Mighty Messenger, Life Carrier, Melchizedek, Chief of Seraphim, Midwayer Commission, etc.) claimed to be superhuman personalities. And the more I studied this book, the more plausible those claims became. The information and imagination behind it were so vast that I questioned whether any man or group of men could have developed this material without supernatural aid.

The most attractive thing about this book was the way it synthesized all the diverse elements I had been studying into a coherent picture of reality. Unlike Eastern religions that played down the person of Jesus or wrote him off as another avatar, *The Urantia Book* stressed him as the central figure of our planet. But it also included the best of the Eastern concepts that Christianity could not incorporate. I really thought I had found the handle.

Suddenly Jesus Christ was back in the picture. This was not the Jesus I had learned about as a child, but somehow it seemed significant that my thoughts were turning to him once again.

Another reason for my attraction to this new world view was the way it seemed to satisfy my scientific curiosity. It explored scientific and historical issues and offered a grand picture of the universe that was consistent and coherent. Urantia provided an answer to the questions I had been wondering about and fit them all together like pieces in a massive puzzle.

Equally important was the fact that Urantia drew a picture of a moral universe, and this was one of the things I was craving. I thought this was the end of my quest, and the timing appeared to be perfect. This was just at the time when my inspiration had been flagging. I was disillusioned and tired of searching; I wanted my songs to reflect something found, not the process of groping after truth. Beset by discouragement, it grew increasingly difficult for me to write, because I had nothing solid to write about. But I believed that my discovery of *The Urantia Book* would change all that.

This imposing tome was first published in 1955 by the Urantia Foundation, a Chicago-based educational foundation. This foundation was formed in 1950 by the original group of thirty-six people who had been studying the 196 papers in the book since 1934. The primary purpose of the Urantia Foundation is "to perpetually preserve inviolate the text of The URANTIA Book."[2] In addition to the Foundation, there is also the Urantia Brotherhood and a number of Urantia Societies which consist of groups of ten or more people who meet to study and discuss the doctrines of Urantia.[3] Although over 100,000 copies of *The Urantia Book* have been sold since 1955, there are only about 1,000 active members in these societies;[4] so it is little wonder that I did not run into other students of this book. For some reason, I did not approach the Urantia Brotherhood to find the nearest Society.

This book describes itself as a revelation from superhuman beings that is designed to assist people in "the age-long process from animal to angel and from angel to spirit and from spirit to God."[5] It claims to be a much more complete revelation than anything previously given. But it does not say that it contradicts the New Testament, only that it supersedes it. Biblical revelation is portrayed as having been corrupted, lost and diluted over the years, and part of the purpose of this new revelation is to make the pure gospel message of Jesus available to all who would hear it.

The Urantia Book is divided into four parts. Part I is called "The Central and Superuniverses." This section describes the nature of God (there are three sets of Trinities) and his relation to the universe. The highest Trinity is called the Paradise Trinity, and this Trinity, consisting of the Universal Father, the Eternal Son, and the Infinite Spirit, dwells on the Isle of Paradise. There are six concentric ellipses that encircle this central Isle. The first of these is called Havona, and it is the Central Universe. The next level is the Grand Universe, which consists of seven inhabited superuniverses. Each of these superuniverses contains about 700,000 local universes. Our local universe is called *Nebadon,* and it "is one of the newer creations in *Orvonton,* the seventh superuniverse."[6] Our own planet, Urantia, is one of many inhabited planets in the Nebadon local universe.

The remaining four ellipses are the first through the fourth outer space levels. A wide range of evolving spiritual beings inhabits this universe of universes, all in different developmental stages.

Part II is a description of Nebadon, our local universe. Like the myriads of other local universes, Nebadon is populated by many orders of spiritual and angelic beings, including the Sons of God, the Life Carriers, Archangels, and Seraphic Hosts. There is also a description of the inhabited worlds and of the "Planetary Adams" and the "Lucifer Rebellion."

The history of Urantia (the planet earth) is the subject of Part III. This is a comprehensive and detailed account of the history of our planet, tracing the evolutionary development of its life forms. The cultural, moral and spiritual development of the various races of mankind are also chronicled in this section, along with an evaluation of the major religions of the world. As before, there is a description of the orders and strata of spiritual beings—in this case, the ones who are pertinent to the planet Urantia. This part culminates with the incarnation of "Christ Michael" on Urantia. Jesus of Nazareth is really Michael of Nebadon; each local universe is ruled by a "Creator Son," and each of these Creator Sons is a member of the Order of Michael. So Jesus is not the Eternal Son, but one of many local universe sovereigns.

Part IV, an account of the life and teachings of Jesus, claims to fill in all the details that the Gospels omit. It gives a year-by-year chronicle of his life from birth and includes many discourses and events that can be found nowhere else. Throughout this section, the mission and teachings of Jesus are portrayed in a very different light from that found in the New Testament. Jesus' real message, according to this book, is the fatherhood of God and the brotherhood of man. Part IV also includes a history of the early church and argues that it progressively distorted the original revelation of Jesus. *The Urantia Book* concludes with a summary of the religion of Jesus.

Thus, the basic theme of this book is the proclamation that all men are indwelt by divinity and are involved in a very gradual process of achieving complete God-consciousness. All personalities are progressively evolving through various spiritual hierarchies throughout the universe and from one universe to another. Because the spark of divinity is present in intelligent life forms, this process of spiritual evolution will inexorably carry the secret of truth through ever higher celestial levels to the goal of unity with the Paradise Trinity. Essentially this concept is very similar to the Hindu teaching of progressive physical and spiritual development over the course of many lives in the soul's journey to union with the Absolute. It also has several parallels with Greek gnosticism, because both systems involve a whole series of emanations of spirit beings, and both teach that emancipation from mortality is achieved through the application of hidden knowledge. But the Urantia teachings are so all-encompassing and elegant that I was far more attracted to them than to anything I had previously encountered.

I often wondered about the authorship of the 196 papers in this book. It claims to be a revelation from a wide range of spiritual beings that was transmitted by several receptive individuals on our planet, evidently in the early 1930s. But apart from provocative names like Brilliant Evening Star, Archangel and Mighty Messenger, nothing further can be known about the authors.

The origin and much of the content of this book is shrouded in mystery. It often uses terms of condescension as it assures the reader that many of its concepts are beyond human comprehension. A portion of the Foreword illustrates this:

> Successive planetary revelations of divine truth invariably embrace the highest existing concepts of spiritual values as a part of the new and enhanced co-ordination of planetary knowledge. Accordingly, in making these presentations about God and his universe associates, we have selected as the basis of these papers more than one thousand human concepts representing the highest and most advanced planetary knowledge of spiritual values and universe meanings. Wherein these human concepts, assembled from the God-knowing mortals of the past and the present, are inadequate to portray the truth as we are directed to reveal it, we will unhesitatingly supplement them, for this purpose drawing upon our own superior knowledge of the reality and divinity of the Paradise Deities and their transcendent residential universe.

> We are fully cognizant of the difficulties of our assign-
> ment; we recognize the impossibility of fully translating the
> language of the concepts of divinity and eternity into the
> symbols of the language of the finite concepts of the mortal
> mind. But we know that there dwells within the human
> mind a fragment of God. . . .[7]

The language, imagination and structure of *The Urantia Book* tend to awe the reader, and this adds further to the element of mystery.

After several months of study, I began to realize that I did not know what to do with the message of this book. How could I apply it, and what effect would it have on my life? If it only appealed to my mind as a cleverly woven intellectual system, it would not be enough. I decided that one thing I could do was to proclaim this new revelation to others. For the first time I actually began to proselytize people. I called friends on the phone, told them where they could buy the book, and some-times bought it for them. I also bought Clyde Bedell's *Concordex of the Urantia Book* to delve more deeply into the Urantia teach-ings and find quotations that would help me communicate these teachings to others.

Since *The Urantia Book* was generally found in the occult sections of bookstores, I started to notice other things that had similar doctrines. There were a number of books like *The Keys of Enoch* and *The Aquarian Gospel of Jesus Christ* that presented many of the same spiritual concepts. The question of why so many of these doctrines were the same began to enter my mind, and I wondered where they came from. But I quickly brushed these thoughts aside and returned to the supremacy of the Urantia revelation.

I often told people that through Urantia they could know what Jesus was really like and learn what really happened. I accepted the Urantia claim that the Bible had muddled up the true life and teachings of Christ. I thought the Bible was a very limited revelation of Christ and that it was plagued by historical inaccuracies.

The Urantia world view also began to influence my music, and it surfaced in "A Glimpse of Home," one of the songs on our *Monolith* album. This song was about Christ, but it was the Christ of *The Urantia Book,* not the Bible.

When I was very young so many songs were sung
So much wasted time on an uphill climb
But you were always there, a feeling in the air
There was nothing to fear you were so near
Now you are here once again
As I stand in your presence
I can feel the quiet patience of your gaze
Like an old superstition
You are haunting all my dreams and waking days.

(Chorus)

All my life I knew you were waiting,
    revelation anticipating
All is well, the search is over,
    let the truth be known
Let it be shown (Give me A Glimpse of Home)

There's no resisting you among the chosen few
It's so hard to be sure, it's so hard to endure
And when I hear your voice
I know I have the choice
To pursue an ideal, something so real
Now I've got nothing to lose
As I see your reflection
All the answers I desire become so clear
Like a page that is turning
I can look into the future without fear

You're in my rock and roll, You're in my very soul
Though it's heavy to bear, it's a feeling so rare
And it's a mystery, the way it's meant to be
Can we ever know, we're moving so slow
There ain't enough time in the world
As I reach up the ladder
There is something ever higher to perceive
Like a fire that is burning
In my heart I know I surely must believe[8]

It's tremendously ironic for me to look back at these lyrics. I was convinced that "All is well, the search is over," and that my previous years of "wasted time" would now be replaced by years of spiritual fulfillment. How could I have known that only a few months after I wrote this song I would come to meet the true source of joy? And yet the title turned out to be prophetic; I had only received a *glimpse* of home, though I thought at this time that I had arrived. On one level I believed I was inside; but on a deeper level I knew that I was really standing on the doorstep, waiting for someone to let me in.

THE DOOR
OPENS AT LAST

By 1979 Kansas had become one of the most successful and respected rock bands in the country. I enjoyed a real sense of artistic fulfillment, my marriage was going well, I had achieved financial prosperity, and I thought I had discovered the real meaning of life as a Urantian. There was no reason to believe that something else would come along that would absolutely bowl me over. My mind was closed to such a possibility. The summer tour of 1979 changed all that.

The tour started in Huntsville, Alabama, and our opening group for a large portion of the tour was called Louisiana's Le Roux. We had played with them once before about a year earlier, and I had taken little notice of them. Backstage we scarcely said hi to each other, and then we were both off into the sunset. But this time things turned out very differently.

We soon got acquainted with the members of Le Roux, and I often watched their opening act. I was particularly impressed with Jeff Pollard, their lead singer. After two or three weeks another band opened for us, and we didn't work with Le Roux again until late in the tour.

When they rejoined us, we were playing in Rapid City, South Dakota. Just before our sound check, a nine-year-old boy came up and told us he was the drummer in a band that was playing at the lounge in the Holidome where we were staying. He said, "Why don't you guys come over and watch us play?" Intrigued by the idea of a nine-year-old drummer, we promised to accept his invitation after our show.

By the time I got to the lounge, most of the members of Kansas and Le Roux had already arrived. I was sitting around when Jeff Pollard walked in and struck up a conversation with me. Occasionally I meet someone with whom I have an instant rapport, and Jeff was one of those people. We immediately gravitated together, and both of us quickly realized that we had an unusual number of things in common in the areas of personality and interests.

We had already engaged in some small talk before, and I invited Jeff to sing on the solo album I was planning to make. As we talked together at the Holidome lounge, the conversation soon turned to spiritual things and I thought, "Wow, here's a great opportunity for me to tell him all about *The Urantia Book.*"

"I understand you're into the Bible," I said. "Well, I'm into a book that I think is just as inspired as the Bible." Jeff answered, "Really? That's very interesting. We should get together and talk about it."

That night both of us ended up on stage with the nine-year-old drummer; Jeff played lead guitar, and I played bass.

As things turned out, the only opportunity we would have to talk was between shows. But the problem here was that Kansas flew from city to city while Le Roux traveled in a converted bus. So Jeff invited me to ride with him in the back of their bus to Denver for our next concert. I was happy to do so because I had suddenly developed an irrational fear of flying. In fact, during the *Monolith* tour I rode in the crew bus whenever I could. This phobia lasted for less than a year and ended as quickly as it began. In fact, I recently obtained my pilot's license, and flying is one of my main hobbies.

The Le Roux bus is partitioned into a front compartment, a middle sleeping compartment, and a rear lounge which Jeff jokingly called The Chapel (the shelves were stuffed with books and Bibles that Jeff gave away).

It was obvious that Jeff was a Christian, but I wasn't bothered because he didn't come on particularly strong or say things I would have considered offensive at the time. We simply had some very interesting spiritual things in common, and I was all prepared to tell him about Urantia.

We got on the bus the next morning (after a helicopter tour of Mt. Rushmore) and went to the lounge in the back. There we sat down at the table and talked incessantly during the eight-hour bus ride to the next stop on our tour. The discussions we were to have over the next three days on that bus would lead to the biggest change that has ever happened in my life or ever could happen in anyone's life.

If someone even hinted that I might become a Christian in 1979, it would have been a real joke. I would have said, "There's no way. I've found something much better. The real revelation about Christ is in *The Urantia Book*." The possibility that this book could be a misrepresentation of Christ actually designed to lead me away from him was something I couldn't even imagine. But as we sat there and compared doctrines, I began to get unsettled. We were engaged in a theological debate, Jeff using his Bible and I my *Urantia Book* and *Concordex*. It grew increasingly obvious to me that *The Urantia Book* didn't just supersede the Bible as an extended revelation. Instead, it was almost 180 degrees away from the Bible on every major Christian doctrine. It either redefined the teachings of the Bible or denied them altogether.

The first question that Jeff asked me proved to be the most basic of all: "What does *The Urantia Book* teach about Jesus Christ?" Jeff used a number of messianic prophecies to show that the person who identified himself as God in the Old Testament manifested himself in human form as Jesus Christ in the New Testament. He was not an angel or a created being or merely a great teacher.

Jeff used a lot of material to build his argument for the historical reliability of the Bible. At first I was bewildered. I had no conception of why some of these things were so important to begin with. Jeff carefully explained to me the meaning and the significance of the biblical teaching about the person and work of Jesus Christ.

He asked, "What does *The Urantia Book* teach about the blood of Christ?" I told him that it was not necessary for Jesus to die that way. The crucifixion was an unfortunate circumstance that had no redemptive significance whatever. Jeff responded that without the shedding of blood, there is no remission, no forgiveness for sin, and he read a number of biblical verses that supported his position. As we went back and forth, I marked my *Urantia Book* and wrote down all the references for further study. We talked a lot about the issue of sin. My understanding from Urantia was that sin is a form of ignorance, something we don't need to have forgiven. Jeff refuted this concept from the Bible and from human experience.

As we talked, I began to notice a very interesting phenomenon occurring in myself. I was proud of what I believed. I thought I had really found it. My goal was to set this Christian straight. But at the same time, I was pulled in a very different direction. Something inside me actually wanted him to be right! His words struck a responsive chord in me, and this went directly against my mind which kept saying, "I'm right; I can't possibly be proven wrong." Jeff was essentially telling me that I had been deceived.

No one wants to admit that he has been taken for a ride. The internal turmoil taking place inside me was bewildering, and as the day wore on I grew more and more upset. I tried not to manifest this outwardly in my behavior, but by the end of the day I was quite alarmed.

Jeff and I continued to pursue this the next day. He gave me a very clear description of the Christian gospel, and for the first time I understood what it meant. Several things began to sink in at once: what actually happened on the cross 2,000 years ago, who it was who died there, and why. And the more I learned, the more I wanted to know who was behind *The Urantia Book* and why this book so actively sought to steer people away from the biblical message about Jesus. As I read passages from it, it now became clear how vehemently they were opposed to Christianity. Almost between the lines I could sense a hatred for the cross of Christ.

Its teachings are very similar to those of early gnosticism. It speaks of Jesus in glowing terms but denies his divinity, reducing him to one of many created sons of God, not God the Son. As a created being, his authority is limited and extends only to the local universe of Nebadon.

The Urantia teachings also deny the virgin birth and assert that the purpose of his incarnation was not to save fallen man but rather to seal his own sovereignty in Nebadon. By doing so, he enriched his own position and progressed in his spiritual evolution. According to *The Urantia Book,* of course, he revealed a higher stage of religion to mankind; but his motive was not to save others, not to shed blood, but to further his own gain.

This book rejects the whole concept of the sacrificial atonement and says that it is an outgrowth of man's primitive fears.

> Jesus is not about to die as a sacrifice for sin. He is not going to atone for the inborn moral guilt of the human race. Mankind has no such racial guilt before God.
>
> The salvation of God for the mortals of Urantia would have been just as effective and unerringly certain if Jesus had not been put to death by the cruel hands of ignorant mortals.[1]

The Urantia Book, in fact, claims that the early Christian church made two great mistakes:

> 1. The effort to connect the gospel teaching directly onto the Jewish theology, as illustrated by the Christian doctrines of the atonement—the teaching that Jesus was the sacrificed Son who would satisfy the Father's stern justice and appease the divine wrath.
>
> 2. The second great blunder of the Master's early followers, and one which all subsequent generations have persisted in perpetuating, was to organize the Christian teaching so completely about the *person* of Jesus.[2]

Thus, this book minimizes the two most crucial teachings of the New Testament, the person and work of Christ. The whole biblical doctrine of salvation hinges on these issues. The Apostle Paul wrote:

> See to it that no one takes you captive through philosophy and empty deception, according to the tradition of men, according to the elementary principles of the world, rather than according to Christ. For in Him all the fulness of Deity

dwells in bodily form, and in Him you have been made complete, and He is the head over all rule and authority.[3]

The Urantia Book is quite syncretistic in its approach to the religions of the world, claiming that all of them point in the same direction. Next to the Urantia revelation, however, they are only pale reflections (in varying degrees) of the true religion: "the fatherhood of God and the brotherhood of man."[4]

The whole concept of sin and judgment is played down as primitive. There was no fall of man. The human race has slowly evolved, physically at first and now spiritually. Mankind will enjoy a glorious future as we come to recognize the God within us—the Father indwells all of us and makes us brothers. The practical result of this space-age gnosticism is that man does not have to answer for his actions. God's moral nature—his righteousness and his justice—is completely minimized. Instead, humanity will continue to evolve, eventually to become a part of the celestial hierarchy.

I began to realize how much these concepts could appeal to man's pride. They certainly had appealed to mine; there was a certain thrill in exalting myself as some sort of celestial being who was in the process of realizing his true spiritual potential. It was with no little shock that I discovered that this was the same attitude adopted, according to the Bible, by Satan and his angels. Satan wanted to exalt himself and assume the place of God. And it was to the pride of man that he appealed when he made his enticing Edenic promise: "For God knows that in the day you eat from it your eyes will be opened, and you will be like God. . . ."[5] This was the true enticement of *The Urantia Book,* and I had taken the bait—hook, line and sinker.

My previously unanswered question of why so many occult books had doctrines that were similar to those of Urantia now began to be answered. These were spiritual counterfeits, variations on the same old theme. In every case they assured the reader that he simply had to get in touch with the God within. If there was any separation between man and God, it was not metaphysical or moral. It was basically due to ignorance of one's true divinity. This was the primary theme of the Eastern religions, and now I could see how all of these gurus drastically reinterpreted the life and teachings of Jesus Christ to make him conform to their world view. The only way they could accomplish this was to rip verses out of context and distort them to support a religious philosophy that those verses actually contradict. Everyone wanted Jesus on his bandwagon, but not the Jesus of the Bible.

It also dawned on me that the two "resurrections" described in *Autobiography of a Yogi* were very different from the resurrection of Jesus Christ. The ashes of Mahasaya and the remains of Yukteswar did not disappear as did the body of Christ. Christ's body did not suffer corruption but was transformed into a body of glorified flesh. In addition, Christ reappeared on numerous occasions to many eyewitnesses (in one instance, to 500 at once) rather than one time to a single disciple.

Now while I was responding to all of this on one level, another part of me kept saying, "My God, you can't become a Christian! What would everybody think?" The last thing in the world I wanted to be was one of those fanatical born-again Christians. Because of my image of what Christianity meant, my concept of what Christians were like, and what it would mean socially, economically and personally for me to become one, the thought absolutely terrified me. And yet I could not deny that in some inexplicable way everything Jeff was telling me felt right, good, clean and wholesome. It was something that I really needed and wanted, but I didn't want to admit this.

Later in our discussions, Bobby Campo, another member of Le Roux, came back in the bus and started to listen in. Bobby has a pleasant personality and he's a wonderful guy to be around. He said nothing for a long time, but then he suddenly jumped into the conversation. He told me that he had been a Jehovah's Witness and described how he and Jeff had debated about this over a period of months. Finally he came to realize that everything Jeff told him out of the Bible was true. It was difficult for him to acknowledge that he had been deceived, and he described his personal hardship in leaving the Jehovah's Witnesses. Bobby's testimony provided further evidence and pushed me a little closer to the brink.

I began to get more agitated and emotionally upset than ever. It was as though a thousand pounds was weighing down on my shoulders. I knew I was heading toward a significant conclusion, but I didn't know what it would be. I was resisting a confrontation with the cross of Christ, but now I was forced to deal with it. I had to decide on the basis of a lot of evidence that I was hearing for the first time what that cross really meant and who Jesus Christ really was. His claims were so radical that once understood, they could not be ignored. They had to be accepted or rejected.

A person must listen to the words of Christ's gospel with more than his ears. They require a heart response. If one chooses to listen in this way those words speak with immense power, and that power was something I could not deny. Jesus once said to the crowd in the Jerusalem temple, "If any man is willing to do His will, he shall know of the teaching, whether it is of God, or whether I speak from Myself."[6]

I knew that I was really onto something more crucial than anything I had ever faced before. I can't recall everything that Jeff, Bobby and I talked about for three days in the back of the bus, but I know that we went from one end of Christianity to the other. We talked about history, archaeological evidence, messianic prophecy, objections to the Christian world view, the biblical teachings on future things, and a variety of other issues.

As I slowly lost my grasp on what I believed, my whole world view began to undergo a dramatic metamorphosis. *The Urantia Book* claimed to be a revelation that transcended all others, but I started to see through its dazzling and seductive rhetoric. While the Bible claims to be the very Word of God, *The Urantia Book* claims to reveal information about God through a host of angelic messengers of different orders and celestial hierarchies. I began to wonder what kind of angels these were, especially because the Bible speaks of a spiritual warfare:

> Put on the full armor of God, that you may be able to stand firm against the schemes of the devil. For our struggle is not against flesh and blood, but against the rulers, against the powers, against the world-forces of this

darkness, against the spiritual forces of wickedness in the heavenly places.[7]

> For such men are false apostles, deceitful workers, disguising themselves as apostles of Christ. And no wonder, for even Satan disguises himself as an angel of light. Therefore it is not surprising if his servants also disguise themselves as servants of righteousness; whose end shall be according to their deeds.[8]

When Jeff read passages like these, I realized that the spiritual conflict was more subtle and extensive than I had ever imagined. *The Urantia Book* intoxicated the intellect and appealed to the human tendency to exalt oneself as the center of creation. At the same time, it arrogantly undercut the authority of the Bible, calling it garbled and corrupted. What basis did it have for making such claims? It seemed ludicrous that a book written 1,900 years after the fact would simply pronounce that the first-century books of the New Testament, based on eyewitness accounts, were wrong. As my later reading confirmed, an enormous amount of recent archaeological and manuscript evidence has underscored the reliability of the books of the New Testament as primary historical documents. In addition, these books were written too early to contain legendary material. There were too many eyewitnesses of the ministry of Jesus to allow serious distortions to go unchallenged.

The Urantia Book gives lip service to the Bible, but it is really designed to lead people away from it. Further investigation revealed that a large number of religious groups do the same thing. They give a nod to the Bible but distort its teachings through the grid of a nineteenth- or twentieth-century revelation.

Jeff gave me a book called *The Liberation of Planet Earth* by Hal Lindsey, along with a Bible. And, of course, I still had my *Urantia Book* and several other books about spiritual things which I carried around with me in my suitcase. After this time of intense interaction, Le Roux completed its tour with our band. On our last day together (July 22), Jeff and I had breakfast in Oklahoma City. I had gone through some emotional experiences on the previous night, and Jeff knew that some profound things were taking place in my life. We found a Christian bookstore, and he loaded me up with some books that dealt with the issues we had been discussing. Then we parted ways, and I went on to Indiana to continue our 1979 summer tour.

I'll never forget what happened at my hotel in Indianapolis. It was about three o'clock on the morning of July 24. As I was sitting on my bed with open books laying all around me, I grew absolutely determined to get to the bottom of this thing once and for all. I wanted the answer, and I knew that the Christian world view could never mix with that of *The Urantia Book* or Eastern philosophy; they were simply too far apart. In fact, it became clear to me that Christianity is so completely unique that it stands apart from all other religions.

I came to the conclusion that if it was really true, I would have to face up to it and become a Christian regardless of the consequences. If it wasn't true, my only alternative was the mishmash of religions I had been dealing with all these years. In my confusion I reached over and picked up *The Liberation of Planet Earth*. This book clearly described the separation between God and man and the steps God took to remove that barrier through the life, death and resurrection of Jesus Christ, the God-man. About halfway through the book, I was overcome as it suddenly occurred to me that I had to quit fooling around. This was it. If this was the real God, then I wanted him. I wanted to know him in my life, and I wanted him to be the Lord in my life.

I put down the book, tears welling up in my eyes, and I just said, "Lord, if Jesus Christ is your Son, then I want to know him. If he really is the living God, my Redeemer and my Lord, then I want to serve him with all my heart."

Most conversions aren't really bolts of lightning, but for some reason a number are quite dramatic. Words fall pitifully short when I try to describe what took place after that prayer. I was overwhelmed. Laughing and crying at once, I felt that the huge weight on my shoulders was suddenly taken away forever. Unlike all my previous religious experiences, my conversion was based on repentance from sin. I finally understood that believing in Christ means more than intellectual assent; it means turning away from sin (repentance) and choosing to receive Christ's gift of salvation. This time I knew my quest had reached an end—the years of searching were over.

I was so excited that I felt like running out into the hall and knocking on doors, waking everyone up and saying, "Look what I've found! You've got to believe it—this is real. Jesus is your Savior; he died for you." I couldn't contain myself, so I sat blubbering on the bed until the thought hit me, "You've got to get a grip on yourself and get some sleep. You've got a concert to play tomorrow." So I lay in bed, turned out the light, and said a prayer of thanks to God for saving me after all those years of stumbling.

The moment I woke up, I sat up, looked around and thought, "I'm a Christian. I can't believe it, I just can't believe it. I'm really a Christian! Where do I go from here? What do I do? I've got to call somebody." The first thing I decided to do was to try to settle down, go downstairs, and have some break-fast. So I stepped out of my room into the elevator and went down to the lobby. Then something happened to me which almost caused me to lose my sanity. As the elevator doors opened, I was faced with a scene which made no sense to the rational mind: Christmas decorations were all over the hotel. Loudspeakers were blaring "Joy to the world, the Lord is come, let earth receive her King." I honestly thought I had lost my mind.

As I walked out of the elevator, my eyes began to fill with tears as I heard the words "Joy to the world" and understood for the first time in my life what they really meant and what that joy was. I went into the restaurant unable to control my tears. The waitress asked me if I was all right. I answered, "Yes, but please explain to me what's going on." She replied, "Well, it's an annual custom we have—it's called Christmas in July."

Now I don't know if the Lord particularly worked out my conversion to happen on Christmas in July in Indianapolis, but the impact was profound. After I finished breakfast, I got out the Yellow Pages, looked up the nearest Christian bookstore I could find, jumped into one of our rental cars, and raced across

Indianapolis to the store. I had very little time before our sound check, so I literally ran into the store and went around to all the shelves, just piling up a stack of books. I grabbed anything that sounded like it would help me grow in my understanding of my newfound relationship with Christ. As I walked up to the counter with my pile of books, the woman behind it looked at me and said, "You just heard the call of the Lord, didn't you?" I said, "Yes, ma'am, I certainly did." She replied, "You know, every once in a while we get someone like you in here and it just makes our whole week." I said, "Well, ma'am, the Lord just made my whole life."

All kinds of thoughts streamed through my mind as I drove back to the hotel. I tried to picture myself telling the guys in the band what had happened to me. For the first time I didn't want to let them on to something new just to show them how cool I was in finding it. This time I wanted them to know solely for their own sakes, so that they too would enter into this happiness, this joy, this peace, this truth.

I also started wondering how in the world I was going to tell Vicci. That was a major concern for me, because she was certainly the first person I wanted to come to Christ. So I began to experience my first worries as a Christian, and I was bewildered as to what to do with my life. What does a Christian do? Where do you go from here? Now that I've found the Lord, what do I do with him? All these questions immediately began to bear down on me.

When I got back to my hotel room I felt impelled to call my old pastor at the Lutheran church I had grown up in back in Topeka, Kansas. I wanted him to be the first person to hear my news. I got his number from information and talked to him for the first time in at least ten years. When he heard what had happened to me, he was very, very pleased. It was wonderful to tell him that all his labor in me had not been in vain. He had planted the seed of God's Word in my life, and it did not return void.

I had come to the end of a very long road, but this end was in fact the beginning of a much more exciting walk with God that would be endless. And I knew now that he was going to change every aspect of my life—my music, marriage, and relationships with my family and friends. Even if he wanted me to give up music, I was willing to do so, because it would be worth giving up anything for him. I had never felt like that before; I had been a grabber, not a giver. But I knew that this was a God who required all, and I was willing to give everything over to him. Later I came across a statement found in the diary of Jim Elliot, one of five missionaries martyred in the jungles of Ecuador in 1956. He beautifully summed it up: "He is no fool who gives what he cannot keep to gain what he cannot lose."

I felt as though my life was a piece of music that had just reached one of the grand climaxes that I always loved, like those in Mahler's Eighth Symphony and Tchaikovsky's *1812 Overture*. Now I understood why those triumphal moments in music had such an appeal to me. They symbolized my search for a grand conclusion to life, an object that I was reaching for. That object turned out to be a Person; the very Author of life had laid hold of me. Because of this, I had a new appreciation for music. I now saw music as something that could reflect the glory of God rather than exist as an end in itself. The adventure had begun, and it continues to this day.

A NEW BEGINNING

People jokingly say that life begins at forty, and during some pleasurable experience someone may remark, "Now, this is really living." By the age of twenty-nine I had experienced a great deal of what this world had to offer—material prosperity, fame, travel, success in my career, practically anything you could name. And yet I had never been able to say, "This is really living." All these things had been pleasurable but not fulfilling. That fulfillment did not come until my search came to an end with the person of Jesus Christ. It was then that I discovered that true life does not begin until you're born anew in him.

The search I had been engaged in wasn't pertinent only to me. Whether we realize it or not, all of us are on a search for meaning, purpose and fulfillment in life. But every passing day makes it clearer that people can never really be at rest until they are reconciled to their Creator, and Christ is the Creator and Upholder of all things.[1] In Christ we become new creatures, a new species by virtue of a new heredity.[2]

As a spiritual infant, I was perceiving everything in a new light, and I had to begin all over again. This new beginning has become an extraordinary adventure, and the wonder has not worn off. I know the joy of forgiveness and reconciliation with the infinite-personal God. I'm full of praise and thanksgiving to the God who loved me enough to lead me through the mire and entrapment of false religion to him. He's the God whose promises stand firm, who answers prayer, and who remains faithful when we are not. His will is perfect, and he always seeks what is best for us. The fruit of his Holy Spirit (who indwells every believer) is love, joy, peace, patience, kindness, goodness, faith-fulness, gentleness and self-control,[3] and these qualities are man-ifest to the extent that we allow his Spirit to operate in our lives.

My observations have led me to the conclusion that most new believers are given a special period of grace by the Lord to build them up and protect them from the onslaught of the spiritual warfare. But God is not an overprotective parent, and he does not dissipate all of our difficulties. Christians are not exempt from problems, but they do have a relationship with the only problem-solver who can carry us through times of struggle and difficulty and in fact use those times as tools to forge quali-ties of character and Christlikeness in our lives.

The quest was over, but the real journey had just begun. Because of the situation I was in, I knew I had to grow at a very fast pace as a Christian. The New Testament epistles all stress the need for growth into spiritual maturity in Christ. My circum-stances on the road made this need increasingly obvious. The external routine of developing albums and touring had not changed, but internally my values and my whole world view had just emerged from a radical metamorphosis. Like a burgeoning plant, the new life in me had to be watered and nurtured. This was difficult for the first few months because I was not initially exposed to much fellowship or good Bible teaching. I had to rely on literature; so I quickly amassed a collection of Christian books and plunged in. I also spent a lot of time in the Bible, and I read the New Testament twice before dipping into the Old Testament. It was astonishing how much of it I was seeing for the first time. In earlier days I had read or heard much of the New Testament, but now the Spirit was beginning to open my eyes to things that had previously passed me by. Even now when I read the Scriptures a verse I have seen many times suddenly leaps out at me, pregnant with new meaning.

The first opportunity to share my newfound faith came quickly. The band had an engagement in Kalamazoo, Michigan, and my parents were living only a few miles away in Jackson. They drove me to their home after the concert, and I stayed there the next day. For hours I tried to figure out exactly how

I was going to tell them what had happened, since I hadn't told anyone except my pastor back in Topeka. It was easy to tell him on the phone, but telling someone face to face that I was a "born-again" Christian was another matter. But I felt a special need to tell my parents even before Vicci, and the Lord timed it perfectly to enable me to be in Jackson the day after my conversion. We sat up late that evening, and I related the whole story. They seemed quite pleased, though perhaps a little mystified. I tried to convey to them that the Christian experience is much more than what we had known in the years I was growing up. It was not simply going to church every Sunday and trying to be a good person. Rather, it is a personal relationship that begins when someone receives Christ's gift of salvation by faith. Jesus spelled it out clearly: "Truly, truly, I say to you, unless one is born again, he cannot see the kingdom of God."[4] I had never known the kingdom of God prior to my spiritual birth.

A more formidable task still awaited me: telling the band. I didn't know how or when I was going to tell them, but I knew it had to be done. This was something new to me, because I had never felt a need to tell the band about the phases in my earlier religious pilgrimage. In fact, I usually remained aloof about the whole thing, because I knew they weren't really interested in religion. My experience with Christ, however, was totally different. I wanted to tell not only the members of the band but everyone else I came across. I even remember riding in Cleveland on that tour with a cab driver and feeling like tapping him on the shoulder and saying, "Do you know Jesus Christ as your personal Savior?" That would have been considerably easier to do than telling the people I had been with for nine years. There's something about familiarity that takes away credibility. The Lord expressed the same principle when he said, "A prophet is not without honor except in his home town, and in his own household."[5]

As it turned out, I didn't need to make a formal declaration to the band. The fact that I was continually reading the Bible or carrying Christian books or talking to other Christians made it rather apparent that something had taken place in my life.

They all knew that Jeff Pollard was a Christian and that I was constantly with him whenever Le Roux toured with Kansas. Everyone in the band deduced what had happened without my having to tell them, and this immediately became a growing point of tension. The band members never expressed an active interest in talking about these things. I suppose they were nervously hoping that this would prove to be another passing phase. My former pursuits never disturbed them, but Christianity was another story, because of the obvious effect it was having on my life.

I did get into some discussions with our roadies, however, and one of these was an animated debate over the issue of evolution. An English roadie, one of our technicians, had read a book that related to the science and the Bible issue, and he began to challenge me on a number of points. I got frustrated because of my lack of knowledge as a new Christian, and that night I prayed for the answers I would need to meet these objections. The next morning I got in a rental car (we were in Greenville, South Carolina near the end of our 1979 summer tour) and drove to a church about a mile away. When I pulled into the parking lot, there was not a white face to be seen. Not because of prejudice but because of a fear of the discomfort I might have experienced as the only white person in a black church, I decided to turn around and drive off to another church. But after four blocks I felt the chastening of the Lord and knew he was telling me to go back. These were brothers and sisters in the Lord, and he wanted me to be a part of their fellowship that day. They received me with genuine warmth and love, and when I heard the special speaker who was with them that day God's purpose became very clear. The speaker was an expert on the issue of science and the Bible, and he answered the exact questions I had been asking as a result of my discussion the night before.

Knowing that my conversion to Christianity would have no minor impact on my relationship with Vicci, I decided to wait until the end of the tour to tell her, so I could explain everything face to face. I had a tremendous burden for her to know the Lord as I did, but I wanted to broach the subject as carefully as possible. When I finally got home, I put away my suitcases and immediately told Vicci exactly what had taken place. As she sat there, she seemed taken aback and a little afraid. She was kind of quiet for the next few days, evidently fearing that she was going to lose me for some reason, which of course was the farthest thing from my mind. In spite of my intentions, I think I came on a little too strong; I wasn't well-grounded enough to effectively communicate my faith, and I couldn't restrain my zeal. In the following weeks, I discovered that the best approach was to remain diligently in prayer and to allow Christ to live and reign in me so that the quality of my life would be different. Then as God provided opportunities, I would be willing and ready to share the good news about Jesus.

Unlike my conversion, which I could pin down to a specific date, Vicci's was more of a process. Nevertheless, hers was just as real as mine, and the effect this spiritual dimension has had on our marriage has been tremendous. Our mutual commitment of obedience to Christ has bound us closer together than we could ever have been without him.

One thing I found the Lord provided abundantly was a whole new set of friends. Of course, Jeff was the first real Christian friend I ever had, and my relationship with him has always been a very special one since he was the person who led me to Jesus. Ours is a friendship that will last quite literally forever.

Another friend stepped into my life as a result of my browsing around in a Christian bookstore on 8th Avenue in New York City. I was beginning to develop a lot of questions about Christian theology, and I was frustrated because I had not yet found anything that provided the answers I sought. I wanted to know more about the mystery of Christ's complete deity and yet complete humanity, the mystery of the Trinity, the relationship of divine sovereignty and human responsibility, the whole problem of evil, and God's relation to time and space.

In the bookstore, a paperback with a photograph of the Orion Nebula on the cover caught my eye. I reached for it and it turned out to be a copy of *God, I Don't Understand* by Kenneth Boa. As I looked over this book I realized that it specifically addressed all the questions I had been raising. After reading it in the next couple of days, I was so grateful to the Lord and to the person who wrote the book that I decided to track this author down and personally thank him for writing it. The book indicated that Ken was with New Life in Knoxville, Tennessee; so I called that organization only to find out he was teaching at The King's College in Briarcliff Manor, New York. So I called the college and was astounded to find out that he had just moved to Atlanta to work with Walk Thru the Bible. So when I got home from the tour I called Ken and discovered that he lives only five miles from me. We met for lunch and—to make a long story short—we've become very good friends. I believe it was God's hand that put us together. Ken has a very avid interest in music and the arts as well as theology and apologetics; and my occupation as a musician, coupled with my interest in theology, laid a substantial groundwork for our friendship. This book is a product of that relationship.

It's also fascinating how people in Jesus Christ have a foundation for love and friendship that goes beyond any external circumstances. One of my best Christian friends was Dan DeHaan, the chaplain for the Atlanta Falcons. He taught a Tuesday night Bible study in Atlanta, and I found him to be a superb teacher. Dan and I developed a good friendship in spite of the fact that we had virtually nothing in common except our Christianity. But that was more than enough. I realized that with my old friends, we have a common past. But with any Christian I meet, even a stranger, we have a common future.

I learned a great deal from the teachings and writings of Dan DeHaan, and it was a great shock to hear of his death when I was in Los Angeles. He died in God's service while flying a plane from a Bible study back to Atlanta. He was caught in some bad weather and went down. This was the first time in my Christian experience that someone I personally knew who was a Christian had died, and it produced a real sense of ambivalence. I mourned for Dan because I loved him and will miss his teaching. But I also rejoiced in the knowledge that he went into the presence of the Lord of all creation and is receiving a great reward.

One thing that Dan, Ken, Jeff and I all had in common was

a voracious appetite for reading. The Scriptures, of course, come first because God has clearly revealed himself in the Bible, his love letter to mankind. Hundreds of fine books revolve around the Bible, and a quality Christian bookstore is a treasure house abounding in literature that can transform a person's understanding and practice. I'll just list a few of the books that have helped me the most. In Chapter 9 I mentioned *The Liberation of Planet Earth* by Hal Lindsey. This book clearly presents the work of Christ in providing the gift of salvation and tells how a person can enter into spiritual liberation through him. Ken's book *God, I Don't Understand* expanded my view of God and gave me a theological base on which to build. Josh McDowell's *Evidence That Demands a Verdict* and C. S. Lewis's *Mere Christianity* strongly affirmed the historical and intellectual credibility of the Christian world view. *The Invisible War* by Donald Grey Barnhouse opened my eyes to the reality of the spiritual conflict that is going on all around us. A. W. Tozer's *The Pursuit of God* and David Needham's *Birthright* taught me who I am in Christ and enormously helped my Christian life. I want to stress, though, that as beneficial as all these books are, their real importance lies in the way they clarify and help to open up the Scriptures. It would be a great mistake to let Christian literature become a substitute for regular firsthand study of the Bible.

When I was a Urantian, I told a number of people about *The Urantia Book* and encouraged them to get into it. After I became a Christian, I felt it necessary to go to these people and tell them about the authentic revelation of Jesus Christ in the Bible as opposed to the false caricature of him in *The Urantia Book.* I remember telling one Christian in particular who was at a low ebb in his spiritual walk about Urantia. He began to get a little excited about the ideas and started looking into it. When I later came back and told him about the true life I had found in Jesus, he was relieved and encouraged to press on in his own walk with the Lord.

The more I study the life of Christ and the teachings of Scripture, the more obvious the uniqueness of Christianity becomes. Christ's claims and credentials set him apart from every other person who has walked on this planet. Because of who he is, it is never valid to write Christianity off by saying, "That's all right for you if it makes you happy, but I don't personally need it." If Christ's claims are true, they must be true for all of us. If he is right, all people have a desperate need for him, whether they acknowledge it or not. Most people try to avoid the whole issue by ignoring him or by distorting his teachings to fit their preconceived molds. But the incarnate God cannot be so easily dismissed. All of us must ultimately accept or reject his offer of eternal life, and the stakes couldn't be higher.

THREE MORE ALBUMS

It would take another book to relate all the profound things the Lord has accomplished in my life over the last few years. The deep longings that were reflected in the lyrics of my previous songs have been fulfilled in my relationship with "the Alpha and the Omega, the first and the last, the beginning and the end."[1] This is what I have tried to communicate in the lyrics of the songs I wrote for *Seeds of Change, Audiovisions* and *Vinyl Confessions.*

I first began to entertain the idea of creating a solo album early in 1979. Steve Walsh was making definite plans for his solo album at that time, and I knew this was something I also wanted to do. Over the years I had written a lot of material that simply didn't fit the musical style of Kansas, and I realized that it would take an independent album to bring these ideas to fruition. As it turned out, I never did use any of that material; my conversion cast an entirely different light on the project.

My motives for writing and playing music and for everything else I did had completely changed. I no longer wanted to make an album just for my own fulfillment or glory. Instead, I desired to use the gifts God had given me to make music for his glory. As I thought about it, it seemed that a solo album would be the perfect opportunity to do just that. I saw it as a chance to communicate the Christian message to all those who might have taken seriously what I said on earlier albums. Since I had always written about spiritual things, I felt a deep sense of responsibility to impart the reality that I had found.

I talked about this album with my manager, Budd Carr,

and he got the ball rolling with the record company. It was exciting to get the go-ahead to do the record, and I knew I had to come up with the right material. Sometimes I have a lot of trouble writing music, but in the fall of 1979 God's grace abounded. I stayed in prayer about creating the songs for this album, and that prayer was clearly answered. Songs were spewing out almost faster than I could keep track of them.

There was a lot of pressure on me in those months, because immediately after the time allotted for my solo album, we had to begin the next Kansas album. But I managed to complete eleven songs: seven would go on *Seeds of Change,* and the remaining four would go on *Audiovisions.* As I was writing these songs, I felt a certain conflict of interests because I didn't know where to use the best material. I was also unsure whether the band would accept the new kind of lyrics I was writing. But I simply decided to take a stand, communicate the message I wanted to get across, and see where the songs fell. The choice was not as difficult as I had thought, because the seven songs I would use for *Seeds of Change* just seemed to go well together; they had a certain cohesiveness in their message.

The first song I ever wrote as a Christian was "Just One Way," the opening cut on the *Seeds of Change* album. It's often hard to remember exactly what went through my mind when I wrote a particular song, but I generally begin with a concept, follow it up with the music that seems to fit the concept, and then write the lyrics. The one idea that was foremost in my mind as I wrote this song is that there are hundreds of paths that lead to emptiness and destruction but only one way to the true God:[2]

> There's a winding road that leads to nowhere
> And I've been down each empty lane
> Up against the wall, it's the same old story
> I've been around the world but I searched in vain
> Now I see that I've been such a fool
> I was living in the darkest night
> At my feet there laid a precious jewel
> I burned my bridges and it felt so right

Just one way, just one way, just one way,
From the dark to the light there's
Just one way, just one way, just one way
From the dark to the light there's
One way home

I stood at the feet of a hundred wise men
I tried to live my life according to their way
But I was still in chains, and my eyes were blinded
And it felt so good, but I was led astray
All my life I looked for something real
Place to place I wandered restlessly
I just needed something I could feel
And when I found the truth it set me free

Life's a riddle we can never solve, so we
Invent an answer to the mystery
There's a sacrifice that will resolve
The gate will open by no other key[3]

I had diligently sought answers to the basic questions of human existence, listening to one sage after another. Truth, by its very nature, is exclusive, and contradictory teachings cannot be true at the same time and in the same sense. Jesus said: "If you abide in My word, then you are truly disciples of Mine; and you shall know the truth, and the truth shall make you free."[4] When I came to know him, I was liberated for the first time in my life.

The last two lines in this song ("There's a sacrifice that will resolve/The gate will open by no other key") relates to Jesus' words in John 10:7-11:

> Jesus therefore said to them again, "Truly, truly, I say to you, I am the door of the sheep. All who came before Me are thieves and robbers; but the sheep did not hear them. I am the door; if anyone enters through Me, he shall be saved, and shall go in and out, and find pasture. The thief comes only to steal, and kill, and destroy; I came that they might have life, and might have it abundantly. I am the good shepherd; the good shepherd lays down His life for the sheep."

Musically, "Just One Way" was something of a departure from the style I used with Kansas. It was good to experiment a bit in this album, because I had been feeling somewhat confined. In this respect, I was pleased with the music for "Mask of the Great Deceiver."

Satan is called the "ruler of the this world" and the "prince of the power of the air."[5] This song conveys the way he and his forces seek to spiritually oppress and deceive humans in an effort to keep non-Christians from coming to Christ and to defeat the lives of Christians.

> Well he's the prince of the world
> His work is never complete
> Though he promises all
> You'll lie a slave at his feet
> Don't you know the world is his dominion
> Can't you see that you're bound in his chains
> The time is short so take your strength in what remains
>
> He will fill up your ears
> And he'll dazzle your eyes
> But don't believe what he's saying
> 'Cause he's the father of lies
> In your heart, don't you know that he'll betray you
> And in the end he will drag you away
> Till all the world is cryin' for the judgment day
>
> And he's fallen, how he's fallen
> From the height of the morning star
> Though his light's still shining brightly
> It's the mask of the great deceiver
>
> Though the truth has walked among us
> And the words that He spoke will remain
> There's a heartbreakin' blindness upon us
> All our efforts to be free are in vain
> Without the gift of love
> We're lost without the gift of love
>
> Well, he never will rest
> Until his evil is done
> And he don't want you to know
> Your freedom's already won

Don't you know the world is his dominion
Can't you see, he keeps it in chains
Time is short, so take your strength in what remains[6]

I can personally testify to the reality of this spiritual warfare in my own experience.

"How Can You Live" is a song about my amazement that
people can be satisfied to live on this planet without any relationship with God. Now that I've found him, or rather he found
me, I look back on my life astonished that I was able to function
at all in my separation from him.

"Whiskey Seed" was a very experimental song. I have
always been interested in the blues, but this was my first opportunity to express this on an album. This is the only song on *Seeds
of Change* that does not have a specifically Christian message.
"Whiskey Seed" is simply a portrait of one form of human
bondage.

The implications of "To Live for the King" are obvious. It
is a song about devotion to Christ as King and Lord. "Down to
the Core" stresses that on the deepest level, after surface pursuits and possessions are stripped away, every one of us has an
emptiness that only the Lord can fill.

Of all the songs I have written so far, I believe "Ground
Zero" best captures what I've tried to accomplish, both musically and spiritually.

Days are short and time so dear
So very much remains to be done
It's time to speak of one so near
'Til all hearts have been won

The day is coming when men will look to the skies
The consummation of all who realize
We are waiting for Ground Zero

The wall is high, beyond is much to find
A barrier we built so long ago
With fearful hope and a faith that is not blind
From clouds of joy we'll see the depths below

Across the sea and far away, the eyes of all the world
Await the Passion Play
The final act at last begun, the new is born
The old is bound to pass away
No more the turn of the pages
And now the hope of the ages
For all the bondage is broken, all who see

The oracles, the prophets of the past
The miracle of knowledge was revealed
The plan was laid upon a strong foundation
So long ago the future was sealed[7]

"Ground Zero" is, of course, the second coming of Jesus Christ. The Old Testament prophets, as well as the New Testament Gospels and epistles, all anticipated this climactic event in human history and described it in vivid detail. In his first advent, Messiah came in humility as the Suffering Servant. His purpose at that time was not "to be served, but to serve, and to give His life a ransom for many."[8] But when Messiah returns, he will come with power and great glory to judge the earth, and all the world will know. Jesus warned that in the end times many false christs and false prophets would arise, some even displaying great signs and wonders.[9] But in contrast to these counterfeits, the second advent of the Son of Man will shake the entire earth when he appears "just as the lightning comes from the east, and flashes even to the west."[10]

The circumstances surrounding the creation of *Seeds of Change* made it clear to me that God wanted this album to be made. When I began to write the songs, I didn't know who was going to play or sing on this album. God has blessed me with musical gifts, but a good voice was not among them. I have always been frustrated by the fact that I can't sing and that I must be totally dependent on other singers. But there was a way to turn this dependence into an asset. Rather than use one or two singers for the whole album, I decided to look for the perfect voice for each one of the songs. I wanted to treat each song as a distinct entity and match it up with the most appropriate voice I could find.

Before I became a Christian, when I first conceived the idea of doing a solo album, I knew that I wanted Jeff Pollard to sing on it. Our tours with Le Roux gave me an appreciation for his voice; so I invited Jeff to participate in this project. Steve Walsh was another obvious choice, but when he offered to sing one of the songs, I wondered whether this would make my album sound too much like Kansas. It turned out that this fear was unfounded, because Steve did a great job on "How Can You Live," and the album doesn't sound like a clone of Kansas.

Some years earlier, Kansas had toured with Ambrosia, a band that I've always liked and respected very much. I got to know their lead singer, David Pack, quite well, and when I thought about "Ground Zero" he came to mind as the perfect voice for this song. For "To Live for the King" and "Mask of the Great Deceiver," I wanted to find someone with a good deal of power and range but also expressiveness. As I searched through my record collection, I recalled someone who had a voice like that. His name was Ronnie James Dio, and I had seen him years before with a band called Elf. Unlike the other singers, I didn't know Ronnie James; so my manager, Budd Carr, made the initial contact.

I chose Ronnie James strictly on the basis of his vocal abilities. Even though he had begun to sing for Black Sabbath, Ronnie is no Satanist. People have asked me why I included him in my solo album, and the answer is that I saw him as the right singer for two of the songs. In addition, his work on my album gave him an opportunity to sing lyrics which are diametrically opposed to what he does in Black Sabbath. This provided a clear witness to him about Christ.

By this time, the word was out that I was doing an album, and a few of my friends in Atlanta (Joey Jelf, Mylon LeFevre, and John Fristoe) wanted to participate in the project. Suddenly I had more singers than I needed, but I still couldn't find the right vocalist for "Down to the Core," an unusual song. One night as I was working in my studio on the demo of this song, Kansas' sound man, Davey Moire, came over to the house. We were sitting there, and he started fooling around with the microphone. I whirled around in my chair and I instantly realized that he had the perfect voice for the song.

Now I had the momentous task of trying to schedule all these people and see if I could get everyone to come to Atlanta at the right times to work on the record. God really stepped in here, because the people I wanted were all available just when I wanted them. They were all between projects during the times I needed them, and the odds of that happening by chance are rather remote.

Jeff was able to fly in and sing "Just One Way." Ronnie James Dio and David Pack were able to come because they had just completed their new albums. Steve, of course, was available because Kansas was not on the road or recording in the early months of 1980. We used Mylon LeFevre, John Fristoe, and Joey Jelf for background vocals (we always record these first so that we have enough tracks available for all the other instruments and lead vocals).

The only song I wasn't sure about was "Whiskey Seed." I was in the recording studio laying down a rough track so that the vocalists would have some idea of how the melody went on this song. My friend Brad Aaron, who had engineered the previous two Kansas albums and was working on *Seeds of Change,* heard me singing "Whiskey Seed" and immediately said, "That's it! *You* should do it!" I thought he was joking, but when I went back in the control room and listened, it didn't sound so bad. I thought, "Well, it's my solo album, so I might as well sing something on it. I've never sung before, and I'll probably never do it again." But it seemed to work out, and I made it a kind of duet with Mylon LeFevre.

I was a little concerned about how some of these singers would react to the Christian content of the lyrics. I knew that Jeff, Mylon and John were brothers in the Lord, but I wasn't sure about the others. But all the vocalists sang with great conviction. Whether they believed what they were singing or not, they all put their hearts into it. Ronnie James' improvisation at the end of "To Live for the King" was certainly witness to that. Some of the lyrics he added amazed Brad and I, considering that he came up with them ad lib.

A number of interesting things happened with the players as well as the singers. Phil Ehart with Kansas was an obvious choice as a drummer, but I also wanted to work with one or two others. I began to go through my records again, looking for musicians I respected who might be available. Phil suggested Barriemore Barlow, the drummer with Jethro Tull. I didn't know Barry at all, but Marty Rothman, our band's accountant, had worked with Jethro Tull in the past and knew how I could get in touch with him. I figured it would be difficult and expensive to bring Barry over from England, but after I talked to him he was very excited about the idea since he had never worked on any other projects outside of Jethro Tull. He ended up being worth every penny of the cost. Barry flew over and stayed with Vicci and me while we worked out the four songs he played on. The other really obvious choice was to use Robby on the violin. However, I only had him play on one song, to avoid too much of a comparison with Kansas.

I didn't really tell the record company, the management or most of the musicians that *Seeds of Change* was a Christian album. I decided to do it as an experiment to see how everyone would react. So when Barry came over, he didn't realize what sort of album this was going to be. I had sent him a demo tape of some of the songs, but none of them had vocals; so he didn't know the lyrics. An interesting thing happened one night after we had finished cutting a basic track. We were driving back to my house, and Barry seemed to be quiet and pensive. I asked him what he was thinking about, and he said that something very strange had come over him in the studio. While he was playing and in between cuts he found himself praying, something very unusual for him. He told me that he felt the need to ask God to enable him to do his best on this album. I nearly drove off the road. It's amazing that he was able to discern that this music was an offering to God, even though no one had told him anything about it. This led to some fruitful discussions together.

Some of the other musicians who worked on this album were John Thompson and Gary Gilbert (part of Kansas' road crew) as well as Bobby Campo of Le Roux, who played some trumpet and percussion. It was also good to work with my friend Paul Goddard of the Atlanta Rhythm Section. God opened a number of doors for me to talk with people about him as I worked on this album, and the whole process was fun and fulfilling. Best of all, I experienced the joy of creating something for the glory of God. It was like playing and seeing the purpose of music for the first time. *Seeds of Change* will always be a special album to me, not because it was a solo album, but because of what it represents. It was an opportunity to make a statement about what God had done in my life to everyone who would listen.

I can't repudiate all the lyrics in my "pre-Christian" songs because many of them portrayed a genuine spiritual search. I've even heard various stories about people using the previous Kansas albums as tools to open conversations that brought others to Christ. There are also stories of how some of the songs directly led some people in the direction of Christ because they thought I was talking about him in the lyrics. The fact was that I didn't know what I was writing about at the time. The songs were a reflection of my own search, and when I alluded to the idea that there must be an answer, many interpreted that answer to be Jesus Christ.

Two of the songs that had this kind of impact were "Dust in the Wind" and "Carry On Wayward Son." The former didn't provide any answers, but it so explicitly laid out the ephemeral nature of our lives that it caused people to examine their condition and to search for an alternative to the bleak philosophy in that song. The approach in "Carry On Wayward Son" was more positive. It claimed that there is light at the end of the tunnel, even though I didn't specify what that light was.

A review of our *Point of Know Return* album by James W. Sire in the Christian magazine *His* (January 1979, p. 27) illustrates the way some Christians felt the Kansas lyrics could be useful in pre-evangelism:

> ... *Point of Know Return* is a fascinating study in contemporary philosophy. ... "Dust in the Wind," ... takes the human predicament to its nadir in naturalistic nihilism. If we are only matter, we are without value. We are nothing.
> "Hopelessly Human" (the final song) resolves the quest for the point of *know* return.

Indeed this record is not only musically magical—but philosophically mystical. It challenges and propels the listener to consider an altered state of human consciousness as not only desirable but eminently possible.

This record could provide a stimulating jumping off point for an evangelistic bull session.

Because of these things I was hoping that the lyrics in *Seeds of Change* would affect listeners with even more force. To get some personal feedback on how people were reacting to the album, I put an address on the record sleeve to encourage correspondence. I was gratified by the response: hundreds and hundreds of letters kept coming, and about 95 percent of them were very supportive of what I was doing. In almost every letter that I received from a Christian, I was told that believers had been praying for me and that my conversion was a tremendously encouraging answer. With so many people praying for me, I didn't have a chance!

Along these lines, I met someone in Lakeland, Florida in the summer of 1980 who told me he went to my concert a year earlier in Indianapolis, Indiana. He had been praying so fervently for me that night that he said he left the concert in tears. This turned out to be no accident, because that was the day I accepted Christ.

I was especially interested in the letters I received from non-Christians, because I wanted to see how they responded to the lyrics. Many of these letters were real gems because they were from kids who came to Christ because of the album either directly or as a contributing factor. Here are portions of two:

> The album has had a great influence on my decision to give my life to the Lord. It's obvious to me that the Lord worked through your album to reach me.
>
> In closing, I must thank you for using the talent that the Lord has so graciously given you. Your music is an inspiration to me. You don't realize how many lives your music has touched. You and I both know that it is truly a joy "To Live for the King."

P.S.

Please keep praying for others who were once like me, drowning in their dreams. Pray for me and keep your heart close to the Lord. I hate to think that it took me twenty years to really find his love.

When your solo album came out I was interested in the kind of album it would be. Your songs always were more reflections on life than rock 'n' roll numbers. The Christian undertones made me dwell into my soul and try to find the answer to my spirit's calling after a year and a half. I'm now born-again.

There were also letters from Christians who used the album as a witnessing tool with good results. And a number of Christians wrote to tell me how encouraged they were in their Christian faith by the music and lyrics of this album. For example:

I was all alone, with no fellowship. Then my best friend sent me your album. Well, that was in July, and I've almost worn it out already! How it ministered to my deep spiritual needs, and may I say it exactly fits my taste in music! I love blues and rock. And after I gave up my collection of secular rock, I have hungered for something comparable that glorifies Christ. . . . I love the depth and intensity expressed in your music. I have already shared it with many of our unsaved friends. They really liked it, and one friend borrowed it for two weeks. I feel that we do not have to beat people over the head with our Bibles. We need love and a life that exhibits Christ. I am glad that you were led to speak about Christ, but in a subtle way. Because of that, you can be sure it is making its way into many secular homes.

I have been a Christian rocker for two years now. Since I turned to Christian music my life with Christ has grown in a tremendous way. Your album *Seeds of Change* has produced some fruit in my life. I have been able to witness to several people through your album. It must have taken a lot of guts to produce a *quality* album with Christ as the author. Thank you.

I was always excited to think your lyrics were inspired from personally knowing Christ. When I learned
you were a Christian I've been thanking God ever since.
I have a strong belief that God is working hard in not only
rock music but "secular" rock music—a ripe ministry.

These are the things that made the whole project worthwhile and fulfilling. They're worth more than all the gold and
platinum albums hanging on my walls. According to the Scriptures, a human being is of unimaginable worth in God's sight,
and if only one person had come to Christ through this album,
I would have considered the primary purpose for which it was
made accomplished.

A secondary purpose of *Seeds of Change* was to provide a
definite alternative to the general trend that rock lyrics were
continuing to take. The subject matter of the vast majority of
rock songs is an unhealthy exploitation of sex, drugs and materialism. These abuses have given this form of music a bad name,
and I want to be a part of the cadre of artists in the secular rock
field whose lyrics reflect positive values.

The creation of the next Kansas album followed hard on
the heels of my solo album. This was a confusing time because
of the sudden shift in moods. The solo album was a refreshing
project that allowed me the freedom to write about Christ, but
now I had to go back into the framework of the band and face
a situation where I might have to compromise that. It was
difficult, but I chose to move without compromise and continue
in *Audiovisions* where I left off in *Seeds of Change* with only slightly
more subtle lyrics. This was the subject of much prayer, and I
wanted to see how God would deal with the situation. None of
the other members of Kansas had committed their lives to Christ,
so I had no Christian fellowship in the band. I would have to
face the situation alone (from a human perspective; in Christ a
person is never alone).

It was obviously a sore point, but it was never addressed
in the open. The others were well aware of what I was saying,
but their tactic was to accept it for what it was and hope it would
eventually go away. No one ever came forward and told me,

"You've got to stop writing these Christian lyrics." In spite of mounting discomfort, the issue did not come to a head until a year and a half later when we began to work on the *Vinyl Confessions* album.

The first song I wrote for the *Audiovisions* album was "Relentless."

In the time we spent together
Many words have passed between
And the feelings that we shared are all behind us now
'Cause a change has come upon me
And I'm surely not the same
There is so much more than what we feel and live every
    day

(Chorus)

Relentless, unchanging
Though the world is still before me now
I'm seeing forever
I will keep my heart and mind with you
So joyously I'm waiting for the day

In a single timeless moment
When the old was cast away
The new was born into a world of simple joy
And my life is still for living
Though it's seen through different eyes
And the knowledge of the truth's
A burden easy to bear

It's drawing so near
It's shrouded in mystery
Histories fall, the end of an age
The feeling we're waiting for, hoping for
Now, the time to come alive
The end to which we strive
Will soon arrive

Now the gift is truly given
If you only would receive
For you're standing in the crossroads
And you can't turn back
Though we can't conceive forever

And it's sometimes hard to care
Our lives do not compare to what's awaiting us there[11]

The lyrics are clearly autobiographical—I was relentless in pursuing God, and once having found him, relentless in proclaiming him. "A change has come upon me," and my spiritual birth ("The new was born into a world of simple joy") has caused me to see everything "through different eyes." God's sovereign plan is also "relentless," and this song anticipates the consummation of human history in the second advent of his Son ("The end to which we strive/Will soon arrive"). But each person must come to a crossroads where she or he decides whether to accept or reject God's gift.

In a way I wrote "Hold On" about Vicci (before she accepted Christ). I knew she was looking for answers, and the song says in effect, "Hold on and look for the right thing. The answer you seek is in a Person, and he's just outside your door, waiting for you to let him come in." In a more general sense, "Hold On" is addressed to any person who is on the brink of coming to Christ. Sometimes there's a feeling of desperation when you get that close, and this is a song that encourages persistence (a similar theme to that in "Relentless").

"Curtain of Iron" has both a literal and a symbolic meaning. On the first level, it is about the Iron Curtain, a huge barrier between freedom and oppression. On the second level, this curtain is symbolic of the spiritual barrier between man and God. Just like a curtain of iron, sin stands as a wall that separates man from his Creator. But this wall is broken down when a person finds forgiveness in Christ.

"No One Together" is one of the most complex pieces of music that Kansas has ever done. It was written for the *Monolith* album, and I was pleased with it because I was afraid that Kansas was beginning to shy away from this kind of music. But at the last minute the others decided not to put it on *Monolith,* and this was sort of a crushing blow to me. I was able to get some consolation in the fact that we agreed to put it on the next album. In the long run, this worked out for the best because it gave me another year to think about the song. We ended up rerecording it almost completely, and everything we did was an improvement. In the meantime, I became a Christian and I was able to incorporate my new world view in the song by rewriting the lyrics.

Centuries of backward ways have many left behind us
Who can count the good men gone away
The fruits of all our labors have left us as we started
We've come too far to end it in a day
It seems that everything we do is wrong
A one way trip to nowhere all along
Just look around and tell me what you see
Another stupid page of history

No one together, No one is touching ground
Look at each other, Chaos is all around
Same situation, Nothing is really new
No one together, No one is me and you

Lo the horn of plenty is bursting at the seam
The harvest of the world will be our prize
We claim to know the secrets, the answers have been
        found
But how can one fool make another wise
'Cause nothing's better than it used to be
To live and die is still a mystery
We take away and we give nothing back
We just consume it all and still we lack

Each day passes by us so quickly now
You can feel it drawing much closer now
The signs are in the faces of the people in the street
The signs are in the sounds I hear
The voices filled with hate and fear
You can feel it drawing near you now

The multitudes are searching and wandering in vain
For what they seek cannot be found in men
The truth that lies before us now is plain for all to see
To grow without is not to grow within
For in the promise is a victory
To see the way that everything should be
To feel the joy that we were meant to know
We should have realized so long ago

We're all together, Harmony will abound
Look at each other, All that was lost is found
New situation if our direction's true
We're all together, Everyone is me and you[12]

The basic idea in "No One Together" is man's inability to get it together on this chaotic earth. By our own efforts we will never achieve the utopian scenario entertained by some philosophers and visionaries. Only when Christ comes to reign on this planet will everything come together. This is why the Lord's prayer says, "Thy kingdom come. Thy will be done, on earth as it is in heaven."[13] The first chorus speaks of the present situation with man on his own, while the last chorus refers to the future aspect of the reign of Christ.

In the middle of our 1980 tour with *Audiovisions,* a tremendous thing happened that altered my whole relationship with the band: our bass player Dave Hope became a Christian. I actually had little to do with it. In the first year of my Christian life I spent a lot of time studying the Scriptures, reading books, and trying to learn as much about Christianity as I could. I wanted to learn enough to effectively witness to the guys in the band, but Dave came to the Lord before I had a chance to do that.

We were on the road in the summer, and again we were touring with Le Roux. After a concert in Illinois I decided to ride on the Le Roux bus so that I could spend some quality time with Jeff and Bobby. Suddenly Dave walked up to us and asked if he could ride on the bus with us. Bobby said he had a feeling something significant was going to happen, and he was willing to trade places with Dave so that he could ride with Jeff and me.

Dave was at a particularly low point at that time. He had tried all the things the world could offer, but he was more miserable than ever. He was using a lot of drugs, and he looked terrible. His countenance betrayed the fact that he was quite empty inside.

The next morning Jeff and I were riding in the back of the bus, talking with our Bibles open on the table. Dave came back to join us and immediately asked, "What do I have to do?" There was no verbal witnessing, no proselytizing. He was simply ready and said that he felt the Holy Spirit told him there was something we had that he had to have. Jeff and I looked at each other in astonishment. Then Jeff replied, "Well, just say this prayer with us," and Dave invited Christ into his life.

Dave's conversion was so powerful. To see how far down he had gone and then to see how far up he was instantly lifted was so exciting to me that it was like being saved all over again. I've never seen anything like it—he was physically, mentally and spiritually healed in a moment of time. He was immediately on fire, and he has been a committed Christian since the day he prayed to receive Christ as his Savior. Jeff and I were both in tears to see the outpouring of the Holy Spirit on Dave's life. From that day on, I had a brother in the band with whom I could share and have spiritual fellowship.

Up until this point, Dave and I were completely different in our personalities and interests. I had always been involved with books, religion and the arts while Dave was more down to earth. He had a problem with drugs, drinking and profanity and I tried to avoid excesses in these areas through my self-imposed ideas of righteousness before I knew Christ. We couldn't have been much more different, and yet God demonstrated to us that in Christ we have something in common which transcends all our worldly differences. Now we have a close relationship and a strong bond of love as brothers in Christ.

I mentioned earlier that there often seems to be a kind of honeymoon period between a new Christian and God, a special period of grace before he is sent out into the spiritual warfare. For me and Dave it lasted about three months. But the warfare came upon us, and we knew we had to do a lot of learning. We continued to spend large blocks of time on the road, and Dave and I had to deal with being in an old situation with our new selves. We had to learn how to relate as Christians to the other members of the band and the whole business we were in.

As the months passed, we felt increasingly unfulfilled because a number of things were hampering the ministry we wanted to have. We had numerous opportunities to witness to others because we were in the band, but we kept thinking that something was around the corner that would open up more possibilities. The status quo wouldn't do; something had to change within the band or we would have to leave. Dave and I realized that a gulf was growing between us and the other members of Kansas.

Dave and I went to see The Resurrection Band, a Christian rock group. We saw kids come to Christ at the concert, and we saw them being discipled afterward. The band didn't just pack up and leave; they stayed there and talked to those who were interested in knowing more about Jesus. We found ourselves extremely jealous for that kind of ministry and felt inadequate in what we were doing. (I did, however, have the privilege of recording an album with The Second Chapter of Acts, a very fine Christian band. The album was called *Rejoice,* and I cherished this opportunity to work together with a group of such committed Christians solely for the glory of Christ.)

Because of our frustrations, we fervently prayed for God to do something in our situation that would give us a better platform for ministry. The only thing we could come up with was that it was probably time to leave. So we decided to do one more album. I planned to write Christian lyrics to bring the whole issue to a head and we figured that would be it—the others wouldn't tolerate it.

That's exactly what began to happen, but the final outcome was totally different from anything we expected. I wrote a song ("Crossfire") for the new album that was more openly Christian in its message than any I had written even for the *Seeds of Change* album. The minute we started rehearsals for *Vinyl Confessions,* there was an obvious feeling of uneasiness. Even before any songs were heard and before anything was said, there was an atmosphere of apprehension; everyone could sense what was going on. When I started to show my songs to the band, that feeling grew more intense and got to the point where Steve Walsh refused to sing the lyrics to "Crossfire." He later said that if I rewrote "Crossfire" he would consider singing it. He told me the lyrics "need some work," and I agreed. I thought they could be better; so I rewrote them and they *were* better. But the message of the song didn't change; if anything, it was clarified. Steve looked at the new lyrics and said, "I can't sing this." This started to happen with other songs as well, and we had a real problem.

Everything finally came to a head when we called a meeting to specifically address this problem. Oddly enough, Steve couldn't be there because of sickness. So the rest of us had a long, spirited discussion about what the band stood for and what was being said. Dave and I took the stance that we had one reason for living and for making music, and that everyone could expect that all my music would continue to reflect the Christian world view regardless of the subject matter of the songs.

This was not what they wanted to hear, but I'm sure they expected it. There was at least some relief that everything was finally out in the open; there would be no more subtle innuendos and underlying feelings of uneasiness.

Steve came back and, after another confrontation about lyrics, we started rehearsing again. But things continued to get more uncomfortable. The next day Steve walked into rehearsal and shocked us all. He said, "I quit. I can't do this anymore—this isn't going to work. Good-bye." It all happened that fast, and we were stunned. Steve had quit the band twice before, once during *Point of Know Return* and again during our live album *Two for the Show.* Both times we talked him into returning, but this time all of us knew he would not come back. There had been problems before, but the Christian lyrics were the final straw. It's an astonishing thing that Steve walked away from fame, a large income, and a position of esteem to avoid singing lyrics about the Lord.

The five of us immediately held a meeting to determine whether Kansas was going to continue. Phil, Rich and Robby had to face the fact that if Kansas continued to exist, the Christian element would remain a part of the band. This was something they would have to live with.

Dave and I realized a whole new horizon had been opened up to us, and we started to pray that God would provide a Christian replacement. God had prepared a solution we didn't even dream of, and we began to think we might not have to leave Kansas after all. If we could get a Christian lead singer, Kansas could really represent Christ in the secular music field.

The band committed to go ahead with the album. We had already paid a deposit for the recording studio in Los Angeles, and we had also hired a producer. So we flew out to Los Angeles and recorded the four songs I had prepared for the album. When Steve left, he took his new songs with him; so we only had half an album. Thus, we needed not only a singer but also a songwriter. Because of the uniqueness of Kansas, we knew it would be a difficult task to find someone who could fill Steve's shoes vocally as well as create songs that are up to the standards we demand.

We started to audition numerous singers, and I think we tried about thirty people in all. Out of this large array of singers, three turned out to be Christians. Taped auditions were going on in the Atlanta studio, and one of the tapes we received was from a singer named John Elefante. As soon as we heard him we knew he was our vocalist, but we wondered about his songs. He sent us a tape of his songs as well, and they sounded very promising. All of us agreed that John was the singer/songwriter we were looking for. He was the best choice for the job; so I called him up just to get acquainted and told him we were interested. The first thing he said to me was, "You know, Kansas is the only band I would want to join because of the Christian influence in your group." My heart nearly leapt out of my chest and I asked, "You mean you're a Christian?" John answered, "Yeah, I sure am." I nearly passed out from the shock. I felt a little guilty because I was so surprised when God answered my prayer; I should have been trusting him to work out the situation. Now Kansas has a Christian lead singer and another writer.

It was fascinating that one of the runners-up for the job, Warren Ham, was also a Christian, and we ended up hiring him as a side man to play saxophone, flute and harmonica because we had included these instruments on the album to get a different flavor. We realized we would need to get another musician for our live performances who could play all those instruments and sing vocal harmony, and Warren was the only one who could do all four.

Mike Gleason was the third Christian who sent us an audition tape, and he ended up moving to Atlanta to join a band called Relayer, headed up by Dan Hoeflinger, a good friend of mine. So all three Christians that we tried out ended up here. The odds against that happening by coincidence are rather astronomical.

I believe that *Vinyl Confessions* is the first Kansas album that was truly blessed. Like *Seeds of Change,* everything felt very good and positive in the studio. Many prayers were pumped into that album, and the lyrics were sung by a Christian who genuinely understood what they meant.

Phil, Rich and Robby had expressed their concern that if all the songs were Christian, there would be no variety at all. But we wanted them to see that you can write about anything from a Christian standpoint. Some of our songs deal with the issue of making a decision, while others have a moral message. There is just as much lyrical variety as there was before. It is not our intention to turn Kansas into a gospel band as such. Instead, Dave, John, Warren and I believe we have been called to provide a viable alternative in the world of secular rock.

If Dave and I had dropped out earlier to form a Christian band, our ministry would have been primarily to the church and we would have lost the audience that I believe is so vital to reach. This is certainly not a criticism of Christian bands, because that kind of ministry to believers is needed. But the modified Kansas band has a great potential to reach unbelievers over the radio, in record stores, and in concerts. God has dramatically answered our prayers and led us to a unique place. As we now stand, we're in an area where we can appeal to both Christians and non-Christians.

I think there is a parallel in the way *Chariots of Fire* was able to bridge the same gap. This film eloquently portrays an undeniably Christian message, and yet it had such a wide appeal that it received the Academy Award for Best Picture of 1981. If *Chariots of Fire* had been released as a Billy Graham film, the number of people who would have been affected by it would have been drastically reduced.

"Play the Game Tonight," the first song on the *Vinyl Confes-*

sions album, was somewhat controversial. When Steve left the group we suddenly found ourselves short on songs, and it was necessary before we found a replacement to shop around some music publishers and listen to other people's material. This is something that Kansas has never done, never needed to do, nor wanted to do. All but one of the songs we listened to were undesirable in terms of style and quality. But we did like the music to a song that went like this: "Stay with me tonight/It doesn't matter if it's wrong or right." The lyrics were totally offensive to me; I would never be able to play such a song. So we contacted the writers and asked their permission to rewrite the lyrics. We came up with a completely different idea, and the result was "Play the Game Tonight." Unlike the other songs I worked on for this album, this song does not have a distinctively Christian message. It deals with the whole game of bands and concert tours, and the fact that so many kids take these things too seriously. Fans have a way of emulating rock musicians, but from our point of view this kind of thing is ridiculous. We find it objectionable to be regarded with adulation, and in this song we're trying to convey the idea that this whole entertainment business is little more than a game. You go to a concert to hear music and enjoy the show; it's not the biggest thing in life.

"Fair Exchange" is a song about a totally computerized technological society and the totalitarianism that such a society breeds. The process that leads up to it is subtle enough that people are only dimly aware of what is really happening all around them. In this song, the benefits of this technocracy are offered as a "fair exchange" for people's souls. Many people would indeed be willing to give up their human freedom and dignity in exchange for personal security and comfort. Some Christians associate the rise of the antichrist with a scenario like this.

The lyrics end on this note: "Get out of line, we eliminate you/All for the good of the people/Better one man should die."[14] I was thinking of the words of Caiaphas, the high priest who prophesied that Jesus would die for the people. When the chief priests and the Pharisees convened a council to decide what to do with Jesus, Caiaphas said, "It is expedient for you that one man should die for the people, and that the whole nation should not perish."[15]

"Diamonds and Pearls" explores the same territory as "Dust in the Wind" from a different angle:

> The stage is set, the race is on
> To drink the cup 'til every drop is gone
> And when you make it to the top
> The hunger doesn't stop
> You climb the ladder to success
> The way the world defines it more or less
> You find the grass is greener still
> On someone else's hill
>
> (Chorus)
>
> Diamonds and pearls
> Silver and gold
> Soon fade away
> Empty and cold
> Nothing remains of the things that we strive to attain
> Only the love that is lasting will not be in vain
>
> They say that pride's before the fall
> The stakes are high, you know who takes it all
> To make it through the needle's eye
> You just can't live a lie[16]

The material possessions that people strive and live for are all transitory. This is clearly seen in the first epistle of John: "For all that is in the world, the lust of the flesh and the lust of the eyes and the boastful pride of life, is not from the Father, but is from the world. And the world is passing away, and also its lusts; but the one who does the will of God abides forever."[17] In contrast, "Only the love that is lasting will not be in vain," and this, of course, is the love of Christ.

I wrote "Windows" several years ago, but we never performed it. So I decided to rework the music and lyrics of this song for *Vinyl Confessions*. The "windows of the world" are our five senses. These windows can be quite cloudy at times ("Seeing is believing as some people say/Knowing is to get a better view"[18]), and this is why the Scriptures tell us to "walk by faith, not by sight."[19] The nature of this knowledge is not obvious from the lyrics of "Windows," but the lyrics to the other songs reveal that this song is also about Christ.

The title "Borderline" clearly summarizes the theme of the next song. It's about people who are trying to stand in a middle ground when in fact there is no such thing.

> You're a rich man, but a poor man
> With your pockets lined with gold
> Always in the middle neither hot or cold
> And you think you've found your freedom
> But it always slips away
> Nothing ever satisfies, you always have to pay
>
> (Chorus)
>
> (On the) Borderline, you're standing on the borderline
> You're waiting for the place and time
> And living in between
> (On the) Borderline, you're standing on the borderline
> It's gotta be your world or mine
> So which way will you lean
>
> So much indecision
> Leaves you hanging in the air
> You can't remain forever 'cause there's nothing there
> With one foot in the ocean
> And the other on the shore
> You'll be goin' nowhere, 'til you step on through the
>   door
>
> (Chorus)
>
> Now I know your wheels are spinning
> But you never seem to move
> I can see right through you
> So what you tryin' to prove
> And it's not coincidental
> That you're always on the run
> No more second chances now
> The day is almost done[20]

A person either has or doesn't have a relationship with Christ; this is not a fence you can ride. There are too many people who toy with Christianity while still depending on their own good deeds to justify them before God. There are also too many Christians who have not learned the distinction between being in the world and being of the world. There is no real life on the borderline.

John wrote the music and I wrote the lyrics to "Play On," a song about our motivation for playing music. It begins with these lines:

> All of my life, the wheels were turning
> Drawing me near, to something that's burning bright
> The music begins, a song that is new
> Joining as one, it leads me to you[21]

As I reflect back on the patterns of my life, I can recognize how the Lord has been gradually drawing me down a path that ultimately led to him. My earlier songs chronicle how I groped in the darkness of a spiritual night. But "the root and the offspring of David, the bright morning star"[22] arose, and the day dawned with a new life:

> My morning star, has always been with me
> Lifting me up, when I couldn't carry on
> Turning the page, to each song I write
> Leading me on, on through the night[23]

"Crossfire," the last song on *Vinyl Confessions*, develops the same idea as "Borderline."

> Underneath the sky of blue, it's a time of choosing
> Everybody's holding on, to what they're losing
> But it all works out okay, if you give your life away
> To the one who's holding fast, it's a promise that will
>   last
>
> (Chorus)
>
> You're caught in a crossfire
> Of a greater love than man has ever known
> Caught in a crossfire
> And you've got to choose which way you're gonna go

Caught in a crossfire
In a world of darkness turn to the light

Time's disappearing, all that you're fearing
Dreamers awaken, chances are taken away
There isn't any in-between, there's no escaping
If you step across the line, it's illuminating
And the words are clear and true
And they all were meant for you
For you harvest what you sow, so where you gonna go

(Chorus)

There's no pretending no other ending
All is forgiven, if you are living anew
Everybody faces it, now or later
You can't get around it, 'cause it's human nature
And deep within the hardest heart
There is something there that knows
There's a hunger life can never fill
'Til you face the one who rose

(Chorus)

Time's disappearing, all that you're fearing
Dreamers awaken, chances are taken
There's no pretending no other ending
All is forgiven, if you are living anew, living anew[24]

God's love for us far excels any human expressions of love:

For while we were still helpless, at the right time Christ
died for the ungodly. For one will hardly die for a righ-
teous man; though perhaps for the good man someone
would dare even to die. But God demonstrates His own
love toward us, in that while we were yet sinners, Christ
died for us.[25]

This kind of love requires a response on our part, for it
must be accepted or rejected. "There isn't any in-between"—
this is a decision that each one of us must finally make, and our
destinies hang in the balance.

Even at the time of this writing, *Vinyl Confessions* has already
borne spiritual fruit. For example, I just heard of one person

from Wichita, Kansas who got down on his knees and received Christ as his Savior as a result of listening to "Crossfire." I also hope that this album will be used by Christians as a witnessing tool to communicate the message about Jesus to their friends.

John wrote the lyrics for the remaining three songs on the album. "Right Away" is an unusual song for Kansas because it is basically a boy/girl love song. But "Chasing Shadows" corresponds well with the theme of "Diamonds and Pearls," and the message of "Face It" is essentially the same as that of "Borderline" and "Crossfire." The unifying idea in this album is the temporal versus the eternal and everyone's need to make the most crucial decision of their lives—to receive or reject Jesus Christ. This decision may be active or passive, but it cannot be avoided. The failure to actively choose to believe in Christ is in itself a choice to reject him.

THE ART OF ROCK

One of the first things that comes to mind when I hear the word *art* is the word *craftsmanship*. Even though Christian art and music is often plagued by mediocrity, the Christian world view supports and demands the highest level of craftsmanship. Israel's tabernacle abounded in representational art, and God's requirements for its construction were so great that he had to fill the workers with "the Spirit of God, in wisdom, in understanding and in knowledge and in all craftsmanship."[1] The result was exquisite workmanship in gold, silver, bronze, gem cutting, wood carving, engraving, design and embroidery. The same was true on a more elaborate scale of the Solomonic temple; it was filled with beauty. The poetry of the Bible is also marked by great craftsmanship, and much of it was set to excellent music.

The Scriptures provide a real basis for artistic craft and beauty. God's children are a new creation because of the redemptive work of Christ. He has given us the imagination and ability to be subcreators, to shape our world and create new realms. All artistic activity is to be under the Lordship of Christ for the glory of God. With a renewed imagination, the Christian can soar beyond the stars and achieve a vision of the new heaven and new earth that God promises. In his art a Christian can fuse the present reality with a vision of the future and "see *through* the world to what it could be and, God tells us, will one day become."[2]

The title of a book by Oswald Chambers sums it up well:

My Utmost for His Highest. Even before I became a Christian, I felt driven to achieve quality in my music, though I didn't know for whom I was performing my utmost. *Quality* has always been a key word for me, and this is why *Zen and the Art of Motorcycle Maintenance* struck such a deep chord when I read it. When I later realized that Christ is the source of true quality, everything came together.

Instead of catering to the lowest common denominator, art should have a transcendent quality. Unfortunately, Western art in the last two centuries has, in a general sense, been undergoing a tremendous downward trend. The humanism of the Enlightenment gradually led to the loss of a Christian base in European and American culture, and this has been reflected in art, music and literature. In all too many cases, craftsmanship has been replaced by chaos in the arts. An illustration of this in my own field is the trend toward minimalism in rock music. The idea here is, the less thought, complexity and skill that goes into the music, the better. This kind of approach is totally alien to my nature. (Minimalism is not the same thing as simplicity; it is more of an attitude that results from a largely nihilistic world view. There can be profound beauty in simplicity.)

Abuses like minimalism and lurid lyrics have caused many people to flatly reject the validity of rock as a musical form. Some writers in the Christian community have argued that this kind of music is inherently evil. Now I do believe that music can reach a point where it is so unharmonious, unpleasant and alien to God that it cannot give him glory. Pure cacophony and chaos can hardly represent anything good or godly. Any musical genre can be abused, and this is certainly true of rock 'n' roll. But this does not mean that all rock music is worthless; to say so would be like throwing out the baby with the bathwater. Someone may not personally like any kind of rock music, but this is a matter of taste. A personal dislike does not justify anyone in saying that the thing he dislikes is incapable of bringing glory to God.

While rock music places a lot of emphasis on rhythm, it has harmonic structure, melody and all the other elements that can be found in other forms of music. Some critics focus on the beat and claim that it had its origins in the tribal music of Africa.

Steve Lawhead effectively counters this criticism in his thoughtful and well-balanced book *Rock Reconsidered*. He shows that this is a complete falsehood; the banjo, not the drum, was the chief musical instrument of the slaves.

> Much that has been written against rock music is actually disguised racial hatred: racism. The words used to describe it display this fact—"jungle music," "black boogie," "demon beat" and so on. There was a time when Whites discouraged rock 'n' roll shows for the simple fact that they drew both Black and White audiences. Concerned parents did not want their children mixing with other children of another race who were the same age.
>
> As for the charge that rock's rhythm is demon inspired, most people overlook the fact that in other places where New World slaves landed (Jamaica, Haiti, the islands of the West Indies) nothing close to rock ever evolved. If the beat was so powerful and so much a part of the musical make-up of these people, why didn't something like rock develop in the Caribbean as well? Or, to put it the other way around, why don't calypso or reggae, the popular musical styles of the islands, utilize the same rhythms?
>
> That rock and its "evil beat" originated with the slaves of Africa is a racist notion which will not stand up.[3]

There is also the criticism that the "syncopated beat" in some rock music can "short-circuit centuries of refinement and sophistication, exciting our baser primitive instincts."[4] But as Lawhead writes, "Rock frenzies are self-induced, not rhythm induced, and each listener can choose how to react. Music does have power to move, but not to override normal sensibilities."[5] Some of the arguments that people have raised in this area are patent nonsense. The whole universe is full of rhythm; our hearts beat in rhythm, we walk in rhythm, there is a rhythm to our solar system and galaxy. It's also interesting that the hymns sung even in the most conservative churches are highly rhythmic.

Other criticisms of rock music include immoral lyrics, worldliness and sensuality. I would be the first to acknowledge that the majority of rock lyrics are ungodly and immoral. They portray sex, drugs and rock 'n' roll as ends in themselves. Several rock groups are actively involved in the occult as well, and this surfaces in their music. Some groups in fact openly and blatantly talk about Satanism. But once again, the musical genre itself is not evil. Lyrical salaciousness is frequently found in country and western songs and pop songs. Furthermore, the liberetti of many operas exalt adulterous and even incestuous relationships. Such misuses are problems, but they do not make these musical forms evil. The fact is that any musical genre can be used to honor or defame the name of God. The history of art and music reveals that styles are constantly changing. These artistic styles are neither godly or ungodly, just different. The conservative Christian community unfortunately has a tendency to automatically reject new styles as unsuitable (only later to tolerate, then embrace the same styles and techniques).

Most people are not aware of the need to evaluate all artistic work on several levels. When they see a film, go to a play, hear a concert, read a book, or look at a painting, they simply walk away with a vague notion of why they either liked or disliked it. It is important to approach the arts in a more thoughtful and critical way than this.

In his insightful little book *Art and the Bible,* Francis Schaeffer offers four basic standards of judgment that a Christian should use when considering a work of art.[6] The first standard is *technical excellence*. I may not agree with the world view that is communicated in Bergman's *Wild Strawberries* or Fellini's *8½,* but this would in no way justify my calling these great films trash. They are in fact fine examples of cinematic craftsmanship at its best. Similarly, a rock band may abound in originality, spontaneity, versatility, competent musicianship and stage presence, even though its lyrics are completely objectionable.

The second standard Schaeffer lists is *validity*. By this he means "whether an artist is honest to himself and to his world view or whether he makes his art only for money or for the sake of being accepted."[7] No field of artistic endeavor is unscathed by the problem of the prostitution of talent and creativity. Practically every artist has to struggle with the temptation of compromise to commercialism, and all too many succumb to the lure.

The third criterion is *content*. In their work, artists intentionally or inadvertently manifest their world views. This is an unavoidable result of artistic endeavor, and the greater the artistic quality, the more powerfully the underlying message will be communicated. Great art is far more effective than hackwork in the promotion of both truth and error, morality and immorality. Lawhead adds this comment in *Rock Reconsidered*:

> Good art with a true message is held in high esteem; the message is reinforced by the quality of the art. This is the best, but danger lies close by. When good art is coupled with a false message, the message gains importance. It takes on a credibility it would not and could not and should not ordinarily have. In responding to the goodness of the art, people may suspend judgment and accept the false message, too.[8]

A Christian must critically weigh the content of the art and music he is exposed to in light of his beliefs. He may appreciate the work from a standpoint of technical excellence and even validity, but if the content is inimical to Christianity, he owes it to himself to be aware of this. He must guard against confusion at this point; a positive response on the technical level should not be confused with a positive response on the content level. Conversely, we should distinguish a negative technical response from a negative content response. Some Christian musicians write lyrics that speak well of God's work in Christ and perform for his praise, but their music may be poor, absolutely mediocre. In this case, I must take care not to confuse mediocrity with the message. For me it is quite frustrating to listen to shoddy music or view second-rate art that was meant for the glory of God. Validity and content without technical excellence is not enough.

The fourth standard for judging artistic work is *the integration of content and vehicle*. "For those art works which are truly great, there is a correlation between the style and the content. The greatest art fits together the vehicle that is being used and the message that is being said."[9] This criterion should be balanced with the fact that styles are constantly in flux. It is unwise to absolutize older styles and discredit contemporary styles just because they are new. But even within contemporary rock music there are a variety of stylistic vehicles, and some are more appropriate for the communication of a particular message than others.

The music of Kansas is a ministry for me even though it is not a Christian band. This is where we are set apart from someone like Phil Keaggy or a Christian group like The Second Chapter of Acts. In a way I envy them, but when I talk to some Christian musicians I find there is a sense in which they also envy my situation. The difference is that I have chosen to remain a Christian in an organization that plays music that is not totally Christian. Some may disagree with me, but I see an analogy with a Christian plumber or policeman. You don't find a whole plumbers' union composed of Christian plumbers or a whole police force composed of Christians, and yet a Christian in either context could do his best work for the honor of God and bring light into darkness.

Working as I do in a predominantly secular environment, I have ample opportunities to present the good news about Jesus to non-Christians. The same has been true of Jeff Pollard. If he had been a musician in a gospel band, the chances are very good that I would not have met him or listened to his music—he never would have got his foot in the door. But because of our common ground and the intelligent and perceptive way he presented the gospel to me, I finally received it with joy. Jeff decided to remain for a time where he was, and as a result he was able to reach me and many others.

The Bible talks about holiness and sanctification, and these terms mean that believers are to be separated *from* the world *unto* God. But separation does not mean isolation.[10] It is clear that the Lord did not isolate himself from the sinners and disreputable people of his day. Christians are called to reclaim territory in their occupations in a redemptive way. Of course, if someone was working as a pornography dealer or bookmaker before he became a Christian, it would be prudent for him to leave such an occupation and seek something more consistent with his new beliefs. But as a musician, I believe I can continue to pursue my occupation and reclaim territory in the name of Jesus. Kansas has sold millions and millions of records, and I have been given a tremendous vehicle to communicate the new life I've found in Christ to the many Kansas fans who listen to what I say with such seriousness. To me it would be very foolish to turn around and walk away from that kind of opportunity. The day may come when this vehicle for ministry exhausts itself, and if that should happen I will quickly seek God's leading elsewhere.

In saying these things, I am in no way minimizing the work of Christian musicians and gospel bands. This is a valid ministry to Christians, and many of these groups are effective in outreach as well. But the new Kansas band has a greater potential to reach the secular market, and in this way I think we are working in an area where there is a terrible void.

Because of the mechanism of the music industry itself, a lot of the Christian groups' potential as a ministry to reach unbelievers is reduced. The industry's radical separation be-tween secular and gospel makes it next to impossible for their music to get to the unbelievers commercially. It goes directly to Christian radio stations and Christian book/record stores which are frequented almost entirely by Christians.

It is entirely possible, if not probable, however, that the secular system will not continue to tolerate a Christian message within its framework. The gospel is, after all, a stumbling-block and an offense to the world. It is perhaps even more likely that the situation with Kansas will deteriorate from within due to the pressures of internal division, a division our Lord told us he would bring.

Naturally, I want our new records to be sold in Christian bookstores, but not exclusively. Non-Christian kids are simply not in the habit of strolling into Christian bookstores to buy records. Even if all the members of the Kansas band became Christians, I doubt that we would suddenly change our style or record on a Christian label.

The Apostle Paul wrote, "I have become all things to all men, that I may by all means save some."[11] By creating music that holds its own artistically against the best groups that exist, we lend credibility to our message. By communicating the Chris-tian message in a subtle rather than a blatant or blunt way in our lyrics, we hope to maintain the interest and capture the imagination of both non-Christian and Christian listeners.

There is a parallel with the parables of Christ and the way I try to write my lyrics. I pattern them after the parables so that those who have ears to hear will hear, and those who don't will just write them off as something vaguely spiritual.

Where do things go from here? I made a statement on the jacket of my solo album that I had found a new source of inspiration. This was a real understatement, because God is the ultimate source of inspiration in that he is the source of all things. In Christ I find limitless resources; the spiritual dimension opens up so many vistas of the imagination that I hardly know where to begin. The Christian world view relates to every subject, every area of interest and concern. Now when I sit down to write, the Lord always comes to mind; different chord changes make me think of different aspects of his matchless character.

The years of searching and emptiness are over because I have found a relationship with the One I was created to know and serve. He permeates everything I do, and I wouldn't have it any other way.

PART II
(1990)

BRANCHES

The Seeds of Change have sprouted into many branches, and spread in directions it would have been impossible to predict. I have walked nearly as many paths since my conversion as I did prior to it, but these paths are more focused and less broad. I have always regretted the mentality that once a song is recorded, its development is finished, as if the creative process could go no further. Few musicians have the opportunity to re-record a piece of music, regardless of how they may have been able to improve on it since the time it was "immortalized" on tape. Similarly, it is not often that an author has the opportunity to embellish or add to a published work, but that is precisely the opportunity I have been given here.

At the beginning of Chapter 11 I said that it would take another book to describe all the changes God has wrought in my life. That is doubly true now. I have no desire to change or retract anything in the preceding pages, but there is much more to the story than was relayed in the first edition of this book.

Seven years have passed since the last word was typed in the previous chapter. So much has transpired that it is difficult for me to find a starting point. When I say that there is more to the story, the first thing that comes to my mind is not what has changed, but what has continued. I am still a Christian, I still believe that the Bible is pure and divinely inspired truth, my life still revolves around the Lord Jesus Christ, and, if anything, I am more convinced of these things now than I was seven years ago. The world is a different and rapidly changing place, and my personal life has taken some turns that I never would have imagined, but my faith in Christ has been like an anchor that holds the ship into the wind. The seasons and circumstances of life constantly change, but God does not.

At my last writing, I was still a member of Kansas. As of this writing, I have just returned from a "reunion" tour of Europe as a member of Kansas. That is actually quite remarkable, since during the intervening years Dave Hope and I have not been with the band. I wrote that if Kansas ceased to be a platform from which I could minister through music, or if the internal relationships made it impossible to continue, that I would seek God's leading elsewhere. That is precisely what happened in 1983.

As I look back, I can now see God's wisdom with clarity. I don't think I did at the time, which for most of us is generally the case. If only we could learn to wait upon Him, and trust Him completely.

It really shouldn't have come as any surprise, but the tension between the members of the band began to increase during and after the Vinyl Confessions tour. The Scriptures make it very clear that a divided house cannot stand, and Kansas was certainly divided. Something eventually had to give. I felt a constant pressure to compromise in many areas, and I'm sure the other guys were becoming increasingly uncomfortable with Kansas being tagged as a Christian band, which it was not. In many ways, it was unfair of me to expect them to be involved in something which, for me, was spiritual in purpose.

There had always been a variety of motives behind each member of the band, but the lines became more clearly drawn after my conversion. I was the ongoing "spiritual pilgrim" of the band, but it had never really been an issue until I became a Christian, and a publicized and outspoken one at that. So we found ourselves governed by different motives, goals, and methods. The band no longer had a unified vision, and we found ourselves facing dwindling record and concert sales. I was bearing a burdensome yoke, trying to deal with the increasing pressure to write commercially successful music which could put the band " back on top," and still be true to my own goals for the band. It always went against my grain to be pushed that way, if only for artistic reasons. Consequently, I went through the worst "writer's slump" I have ever experienced. I was nearly a non-participant in the next Kansas album, *Drastic Measures*. I contributed only three songs to the album, and of those three, "Mainstream" is the only one I think should have gone on the album. It expressed exactly how I felt (and still feel) about the struggle between artistic integrity and blatant commercialism. I had actually written several other songs at the time, but they were either rejected by the band, or I intentionally held them back for a future project. Fortunately, John Elefante valiantly took up the slack on that record as a songsmith, but it was becoming apparent that my days with Kansas were coming to a close.

To be fair, the controversy of our Christianity was not the only reason Dave and I left the group. On this earth, all good things must come to an end sometime, and I was increasingly feeling that Kansas had exhausted itself artistically and everyone just needed a change. There had always been many musical paths that I longed to explore that would never fit into the Kansas mold. Plus, it had been many years since I had worked with any other musicians.

The "Seeds of Change" experience along with working with people like Warren Ham had whetted my appetite to work with other artists. I was also getting tired of the "corporate machine" that Kansas had become. It was a monster with a huge appetite, leaving little time for anything else. The Kansas recording budget seemed to consume our hard-earned money in what I thought was a very cumbersome and inefficient way. I was also re-evaluating my priorities since my daughter came into my life in 1981. It was hard enough being on the road when it was just Vicci and me, but we were now a family. All of these things were pointing toward a big change for me, one which was simultaneously exciting and frightening. My life had revolved around Kansas for so long that it was hard to imagine not being a part of it.

Dave and I began to discuss and pray over these things almost every time we were together. An answer became evident to us about halfway through the recording of my second solo album, *Time Line*. A deal had been negotiated with CBS Records for me to do another solo project, and I had decided to use Dave on bass, with Warren Ham and Michael Gleason on vocals. Both of these men had previously worked with Kansas as back-up musicians. I used a couple of different drummers, but a session player from Nashville, Dennis Holt, really fell into place. I was suddenly emerging from my writer's desert, and found that Mike Gleason could contribute some interesting material as well.

The further we got into this album, the more apparent it became to everybody that what had begun as a solo effort by me was taking shape as a band. Everyone involved was a committed believer, and we shared musical tastes as well. Thus "A.D." was born.

Another major decision I made at that time proved to be one of the wisest I have made. Instead of spending my recording budget from CBS at a studio, I combined it with some of my own funds and purchased 24-track studio equipment of my own, and built a studio into my house. The good news was that we now had virtually unlimited time to record. The bad news was that there was nothing left of the budget for an engineer or producer. That left me to do those jobs myself. I was not too worried about the production part of it, as I had always viewed that as a musical decision making process. The engineering, however, is a technical function, one in which I was not as confident of my abilities. I had been looking over the shoulder of recording engineers for years, but it was quite another thing to attempt it myself.

Although having my own studio was a lifelong dream fulfilled, I realize now that it would take the next four years and four albums for me to be satisfied with myself as an engineer. The A.D. albums don't sound all that bad, but they certainly could have sounded better. The budgets we worked under really gave us no other choice, anyway.

It would require another book to record completely the chronicles of A.D. and the things we all learned from being in that band. We were together from 1983 to New Year's Eve of 1985. Actually, it's a little difficult to be historically precise as to how long the band lasted, because after that night, A.D. simply dwindled away over a period of months. We never officially "broke up" or declared ourselves to be no longer together. The second A.D. album which was the first project we did as a band was *Art of the State. Reconstructions*, our third album, was completed in 1986 after Warren's last show on New Year's Eve 1985, and *Prime Mover*, completed in 1988, featured Warren but not Mike or Dennis.

I can clearly remember the night that we decided to form a band. We were all sitting around the fireplace at my house in Atlanta. We had been talking about it for quite a while, but that was the night that we made the decision. We prayed together, and discussed some of the ground rules and goals of the band. Shortly after that, Dave and I called a meeting with Kansas and the managers and lawyers that needed to be present and announced that we were leaving the group. We soon found out something that would have a profound effect on our new band.

The "corporate monster" that I mentioned earlier proved to be a tangled web of contracts that Dave and I were trapped in. We were literally unable to quit Kansas any more than one can quit the U.S. Army.

It was an uncomfortable and unworkable stalemate, and because of it, A.D. had to make a radical change of plans. We had never intended for the band to sign with a Christian record label and be a "Gospel" group. Our vision of the band was to play and record for the general marketplace—the same crowds that Kansas would have played for. But that door was closed to us since Dave and I were contractually "tied up." Fortunately, we were able to get a waiver to record and perform in the "religious marketplace" as they call it (something about that choice of words makes me uncomfortable). But it was the only door that was open to us, so we went through it. Our management formed a label, Kerygma Records, and we began making plans to tour.

I don't think any of us were prepared for what was to follow. My time with A.D. contained some of the highest highs and the lowest lows I have experienced. It was very humbling after being in a tremendously successful rock group like Kansas to find ourselves riding on the floor of a rented van and playing in a sleazy club one night, and a church auditorium the next.

One of the most painful revelations for us was discovering that the "Christian music business" was filled with many of the same pitfalls as the secular. Somehow we naively expected things to be different. Some of the shoddy lack of professionalism we experienced was extremely distressing, and it was a real struggle for me to deal with spiritually. On the other hand, we found ourselves learning and growing in our personal relationships with the Lord. Looking back on it, it was a time of testing and trying of our faith and our friendships. There were many areas of my life that needed to be exposed to scrutiny, and I never would have learned to deal with those things had I not been in those situations.

We found that the churches expected us to be much more than just musicians; they expected us to be ministers. While all Christians are called to some arena of ministry whether they realize it or not, I was surprised when people suddenly expected me to preach. They did not ask if God had bestowed the gift of exhortation or prophecy on me; it was simply that some sort of message was obligatory, and in many cases an "altar call" was expected as well. This was definitely new territory for us. I had always seen my music as my public ministry, not as a supporting role for preaching. Many Christians view a concert as incomplete unless there is some sort of sermonette in the program. I had always felt that the songs already communicated our message in a much more eloquent way, and did not need to be supplemented by messages from the band members.

Preaching is a primary medium by which the gospel is communicated, but I never understood a rock concert to be a crusade. If God calls someone to preach, let him preach. We simply did not see that as our specific calling.

We teeter-tottered on this issue for a while. At first it seemed strange to me, but after I reflected on the frustrations of being unable to speak out with Kansas, I felt that I should use the opportunity to speak whenever I could, even if most of our audiences consisted of Christians. We were not all in agreement about this, and we finally swung back to the other direction and decided that we were just musicians after all. But we left ourselves open to the idea of sermonizing if the Lord made it clear that we should do so.

If I put myself in the audience's shoes as someone who drove to the concert and paid the admission price to hear a band play, I would feel taken advantage of to be subjected to a long sermon. Many Christian bands are, I think, insensitive to those not of our faith who come to what they think is a concert, and find themselves being proselytized. It all depends on the venue, how it is billed, and who makes up the audience. If it is clearly a church function, or if the artists are commonly known to incorporate preaching or altar calls in their performance, and if God has given them such a call, then I have no problem with it.

On one occasion, I remember quite clearly feeling an overwhelming call to preach a particular message at an outdoor festival. It was the sort of call that requires and validates the action, and in this case it happened at a point in our set where we usually didn't talk. When God is really in it, you have no choice but to obey the command to speak, and you have the oddest sensation of merely being the vehicle that is projecting the words out of your mouth. Someone had a tape recorder running, and many months later I saw the transcript of what I had said that night, part of which is as follows:

"With all my heart I pray to our Sovereign God that you leave this place not just thinking about rock and roll and that you had a good time.

You can do that in the World, and for that matter do it better in the World. But something here is different. We are a priesthood, a Holy Nation set apart from the World. . . .

In the short time that A.D. has been a Christian band, we have developed these neat little speeches that we get up in front of you and say, and it has become quite routine. Maybe I'm just going through—maybe we're all (the band) going through— what all musicians go through when they become Christians. But for God's sake, please don't just come here to rock and roll. I didn't get up here just to play rock and roll. I didn't even get up here to preach, really. I don't know how to preach, I'm not a preacher. . . .

We each have a gift from the Lord to do something. The

only thing that I know how to do for sure is play music, and in my heart of hearts, I want to take that gift that was given me and give it all back to Him. . . .

There are more important things going on in this world than rock and roll. A lot more important things. People all around us are dead in their sins, and when they come here tonight, I pray to our Lord and God that they will know something is different. You've all got to ask yourselves this question: Am I building up and edifying the Body of Christ? Do the people around me look at me and see Christ on this stage? I don't have the answer. I only have the question, and I have the desire of my heart, and I pray that God will answer that question for me and every one of us. Because if Christ isn't in this, then I'm going to quote myself—it's all just 'Dust in the Wind.'"

I think the key to what I said that night, and I remember saying it very passionately, was that this festival was openly billed as a Christian event. If it were only a rock concert, I would have seen it through entirely different eyes, but since it was defined as a Christ-centered gathering with a definite spiritual flavor, I became very stirred when I could not discern any difference. I was not condemning having a good time enjoying music or entertainment per se, but I felt strongly that the people in the audience were somehow straying from the right purpose and priorities in being there.

It never fails to be interesting when you stick your neck out and preach to an audience. The Lord may have had me say all that just for the sake of one person, but many came to me after the show and said that they had been feeling the same way, and were glad that I had spoken out.

Another dilemma that A.D. faced was the natural tension between being both a business and a ministry. This one nearly drove us to distraction, and I have still not found a definitive answer for it to this day. It is a true mystery to me, since it was impossible to fully declare us to be one or the other. We engaged in commerce for a profit, we sold products, we advertised, we incurred expenses, and we were compensated for our services. That is a business by anyone's definition. It would be dishonest for any band to think otherwise, unless they gave away everything and performed for free. But we were a ministry as well, for we preached the gospel publicly and privately, led people to Christ, and our songs communicated Christian truth. There are many requirements for a business to survive, many of which are by nature self-serving. On the other hand, a ministry is by nature self-sacrificing, and done in the interest of others.

A ministry/business will inevitably find itself facing compromises. Decisions must be made which, at one time, will compromise the ministry to insure the survival of the business, and at another time will prove detrimental to the business for the sake of the ministry. The best parallel I have been able to come up with is a Christian book store. This is definitely a business, for it must turn a profit to survive, yet it ministers to us in many ways. Even those who publish the Bible you read probably sold it at a profit. God said "the workman is worth his hire," and I know of no better way to view it than that.

Musically speaking, A.D. was a delight for me. The band had no serious personality clashes or differences of belief to get in the way. We really jelled together as musicians, and some of the most intense and enjoyable musical experiences I have had took place onstage with the band. As a guitarist in particular, I believe my best playing was with A.D.

It's a shame we never really got a chance to be heard. I believe A.D. could have held its own anywhere. We played a handful of shows, but financially we were never really able to make ends meet, and ended up in the hole. An old story.

Long after we had ceased to be active as a group, I decided to release one last album. It was a real necessity because the group was left with some very significant bills to pay, and the royalties from *Prime Mover* were used for that purpose. Almost all of the material for that album was taken from unreleased demos from A.D.

I have no intention of dissecting and analyzing the music and lyrics of all the A.D. records as was done with Kansas songs in the earlier part of this book. There is, however, one lyric I would like to include here because its theology is so pertinent to this period of my life. For me, the words from "Wandering Spirit" capture the daily battles and victories that Christians face.

Wandering Spirit

I've been waiting for streets paved with gold,
Staying alive, but numb from the cold
Drifting away, for the bent of the flesh is to stray
Lord, help me obey

Falling, but His gentle hand
Lifts me again, and helps me to stand,
How can it be, there is so much rebellion in me
Oh, Lord set me free

Chorus:

The lamp is burning, the table prepared
For the wayfaring son's coming home
Oh, Holy Father come dwell in this place
Or my wandering spirit will roam

Father of Lights, no shadow of change
Giving Your life for mine in exchange
Scarlet to white, You have given my blind eyes their sight
Lord, make me contrite

Chorus

On Your cross I died, justice satisfied
With my Lord I rose, and the Living Water flows

The last two lines here are sort of a condensed rendering
of Romans 7-8. I have always marveled at how we who are under
the grace of God can be vessels of His Holy Spirit and still be in
what Paul called "this body of death." What changed lives we
who know Christ would have if we understood, moment by
moment, that our bodies are the Temple of God, the Holy of
Holies. I am amazed that God could choose such an unworthy

one as myself upon whom to show His mercy. Of course, there are none who are worthy, and the more one is sanctified, the more heinous should be one's view of sin. The brighter the Lord's light shines, the more it exposes. That is part of the adventure of being a Christian. For the last few years the Lord has been revealing things to me about myself that, layer by layer, need His touch to be rebuilt in His image. I know that at the moment I believed, two things happened. First, I was born of the Spirit and became a totally new creature in Christ—one who was born of incorruptible seed and is seated with Christ in the Heavenly places (2 Cor. 5:17; 1 Pet. 1:23; Eph. 2:6). But at the same moment, I became a soldier in the war of the flesh against the Spirit (Gal. 5:17). It is difficult to grasp that these two things can be true at the same time.

Paul described it so clearly in the seventh chapter of Romans:

" I do not understand what I do. For what I want to do I do not do, but what I hate I do. And if I do what I do not want to do, I agree that the law is good. As it is, it is no longer I myself who do it, but it is sin living in me. I know that nothing good lives in me, that is, in my sinful nature. For I have the desire to do what is good, but I cannot carry it out. For what I do is not the good I want to do; no, the evil I do not want to do—this I keep on doing. Now if I do what I do not want to do, it is no longer I who do it, but it is sin living in me that does it."

Paul is describing something so perplexing that it almost comes out a tongue twister. For me, this is one of the great mysteries of the Christian faith, as it obviously was to the Apostle Paul. The fact that there is "sin living in me" which has a will and is capable of carrying out this will by causing me to do and say things which I detest is mind-boggling, especially since this body is also the dwelling place of the Holy Spirit who causes me to do the good which I would otherwise be incapable of carrying out. Furthermore, we are exhorted to choose to do good and not evil, and we are accountable to the Lord for the choices we make. So, who is it who actually does this choosing?

Tackling these tough and interesting theological questions is one of my passions. I can sit for hours and dig into these things as I can on no other subject. Often the answer is as elusive when I am finished as when I began. It's easy to see that, as Paul said, "for now we see through a glass darkly." Thankfully, someday we shall see God face to face, and all of these questions will vanish as we gaze upon Him. He has not, after all, commanded us to understand Him, but to obey Him.

There have been many changes in my life these last few years besides the ups and downs of my musical career. Although the focus of this book has been my path to Christ and my musical endeavors, I have had many other experiences. My aviation career, for instance, seems to have come and gone.

I have always been fascinated with flying, an interest I inherited from my father who learned to fly during the Second World War. I obtained my pilot's license in 1980 and bought a new Cessna which I flew for the next five years. Our family took many enjoyable trips together, and I was privileged to see sights that only God and aviators see. I have since owned and flown several different aircraft, but unfortunately, it is becoming so expensive to fly that I recently had to sell my plane. It was one of several things that the Lord has culled from my life, and I bow to His wisdom.

Changes of greater import than this have come upon me—fatherhood, for one. It has always been a secret desire of my heart, and it became a reality with the arrival of my daughter Katy Kristina in 1981. Vicci and I had been trying to have children for several years. Although she had become pregnant, we lost the child each time. That was a great heartbreak for us, harder, I think, for a woman to bear than a man. We continued to pray earnestly, and God heard us. It is said that good things come in small packages, and in Katy's case, she weighed only two pounds. But the Lord saw us through the questionable period of prematurity with no problems whatsoever. He gave her to us through remarkable circumstances, being faithful to His word in Psalm 113:9, "He settles the barren woman in her home as a happy mother of children."

The small package brought big changes. Becoming a father awakened a part of me that would have remained dormant without her. Katy brought a joy and fulfillment to our lives that I would have to say is second only to a saving relationship with Christ. There are facets of my standing with God that I understand more fully by virtue of being a parent. I'm not sure that I ever would have fully understood what it cost the Father to sacrifice His only Son unless I had experienced that love for a child myself, and of course I don't fully grasp it even now. Since God gives abundantly above and beyond all that we ask, He repeated His generosity by giving us a son, Aaron Kyle Livgren, eight years later. There were more lessons to learn, for I never knew that a little boy could so capture a man's heart. My family means more to me than anything but my Lord. I now have to constantly re-evaluate my priorities in consideration of their needs. They are not a burden, but rather one of life's greatest joys. There is an old saying: "Children are the riches of the poor." I am not a poor man by the world's standards, but my earthly wealth pales next to the joy brought by children, and even more next to my spiritual inheritance.

"DADDY, YOU ACT LIKE A MUSICIAN, BUT YOU LOOK LIKE A FARMER"

My daughter, Katy, just stuck her head in the door of my recording studio and made the above comment. It was not an unusual thing for her to say, since I had just come up from the barn in my overalls and started recording a guitar track. I will attempt to explain how and why I made the quantum leap from being a Rock Star to driving a tractor and feeding livestock.

It was actually not just a peculiar change of vocation, but an additional one, for I have not forsaken making music. In a strange and unforeseeable way, these two unrelated activities complement one another.

Through all of my adolescence and adult life I have never seen myself as anything other than a musician. During my college years, I had for a while contemplated a military life as a pilot and spent three years in the Air Force ROTC. What a different life that would have been! But it was obvious that my course in music was set, and I never seriously entertained another occupation until recently. After the demise of A.D., I felt drained and frustrated with the music business. All I had known for years was the turbulent roller coaster ride that is a musician's life, with its all-consuming demands and strained relationships. I was hungry to immerse myself in something utterly different. I really didn't want to give up music altogether, but I wanted to re-prioritize its prominence in my life. I began to pray, seeking what the Lord would have me do. Sometimes that can be unsettling, because one never knows what He may ask you to do, and I think it is better not to ask in the first place than to be shown and then refuse. I saw my career in music as waning, yet I knew of no other way to provide for my family.

As a child, I used to spend part of my summers visiting my relatives' farms in northern Missouri and Nebraska. I always had fond memories of the sights and sounds and smells (oh, the smells!). My Dad had grown up on a farm, and prior to his generation, my ancestors were farmers, so I guess to some degree it's in my blood.

When Kansas was touring, we would drive back and forth across this huge country. Past countless farms and fields I would sit in the car and watch the farmers at work. Something about that type of life always appealed to me; it was so radically different from mine. I always thought of the farmer as sort of an unsung hero, without whom none of us would live very long. Although I had a sort of fascination with them, I never thought seriously at that time about buying a farm and diving headlong into agriculture—but by 1985 I was beginning to reconsider.

I can't recall exactly how I came to the decision, for it evolved over a period of months, and even if I had wanted to sell our home and buy a farm, I wasn't at all sure that Vicci shared my dream. But we talked about it, and she seemed at least cooperative if not totally enthusiastic, so we put our house on the market and began to look for some rural land.

I continued to pray about this decision, and one night I found my answer in the Bible (often our answers were there all the time if we'd only look). I had been unable to sleep, and I walked out into the kitchen and randomly (I thought) opened my Bible. I looked down at 1 Thessalonians 4:11: "Make it your ambition to lead a quiet life, to mind your own business, and to work with your hands." As I looked at that verse, I realized that my ambition had never been to lead anything like a quiet and peaceable life, and to do simple work with my hands. I also realized that what I really needed was exactly that. I made my decision, based upon the confirmation I received from God's Word.

Shortly after that, we found 55 acres of beautiful pasture in Newton County, Georgia, and started making plans to build our house.

One of my prominent faults is that I often barge

headlong into some endeavor without really knowing what I'm doing. Doing that with farming could have been disastrous if we had been totally relying on it for our livelihood. The first couple of years here on "Crossfire Farm" were filled with more funny anecdotes than I have space here to tell. Suffice it to say that we were known in these parts as "Green Acres." The incongruity between my past and my new vocation made it even funnier. People could not (and still don't) understand why in the world I wanted to go into farming.

We got to know our local doctor rather quickly! In the first few months of our new lifestyle I had suffered cuts, scrapes, and two broken ribs, and Vicci had a smashed foot and a crushed sternum (courtesy of our newly purchased horses). I had driven my new tractor headlong into a hidden ravine, sunk it in a swamp, been butted in the rear by a big Dorset Ram; got tangled up in an electric fence, was nearly struck by lightning three times, chased foxes and possums out of the chicken house at three o'clock in the morning in my underwear, planted crops at the wrong time of year, was nearly driven batty trying to repair ancient farm implements; I gave injections, hand-delivered calves, lambs and foals, and sweated more than all the rest of my life combined. But be not deceived, I loved every minute of it and wouldn't trade those experiences for anything. I realized that somehow, this life is closer to what God originally designed people to do. Adam was a gardener and custodian of the animals. Now I truly appreciate the fact that every time I eat a mouthful of food, some farmer somewhere worked harder than most of us ever will just to produce it. I have experienced some real thrills and excitement in my life. Nothing compares to leading someone to Christ, but I would have to say I was nearly as thrilled the day I watched the first green shoots come up in my first plowed field as I was the day I received our first gold album.

I haven't yet figured out how farmers make money. I'm not sure I even understand how they survive. Most of the ones I have met just do it because they love it.

SOAPBOX

I am often asked to comment or voice my opinion about contemporary music, both secular and sacred. I usually decline because an honest response to the question would require a great deal of labor on my part to bring it about, and I'm not sure that my opinions are more valid than those of others. Yet, I am continually asked, so I will attempt to formulate my thoughts in this abbreviated version.

One of the problems in answering such a question is that "contemporary music" covers such an incredibly broad spectrum that it is difficult to know exactly what part of that spectrum I am to comment on. Besides, exactly what are the boundaries of "contemporary" anyway? Five years, two years, ten years, a hundred? One thing I know: the fickleness of American popular music listeners is astounding. Today, a piece of music can cease to be contemporary in a matter of months! It turns stale like a piece of bread. We have divided recent eras of popular music into decades or less, as if any possible social or artistic relevance in a song could not reach beyond that short span of time.

It must be a symptom of our shallow throw-away culture. Things are no longer built to last. Everything, not just music, seems destined for a transitory life, as if designed only for maximum profit, soon to be replaced by the "next big thing." It is as if planned obsolescence has invaded the realm of human expression. Longevity is only relevant as it relates to commercial viability. Quality or creativity seem not, in and of themselves, to be sufficient reasons to justify the existence of a piece of music. They have been eclipsed by something called "image," and marketability, now a necessity for the artist (if "artist" is the appropriate word).

The motivation behind much of the music being produced today is, to my mind, somewhat less than pure. The artist who is trying to be totally original and creative has more than an uphill battle on his hands. There are the necessary (?) legal entanglements to contend with. The artist must not only attempt to convince a record company to distribute and promote his or her music, but is also constricted by the ever-narrowing parameters of radio formatting. If you don't fit the mold, you're out in the cold. Creative or not, if one steps outside the boundaries of one of these commercial formats, it is the kiss of death. One could argue that this is nothing new and has always been the case. Audiences supposedly rioted when they first heard Stravinsky's *Rite of Spring* because it sounded so unlike anything they had ever heard. People seem to prefer to be mindlessly entertained than to be challenged. But even if that has always been true, I maintain that our artistic environment today is getting worse and not better. There is no atmosphere today which can cultivate a Stravinsky. People are obsessed with music at an almost unprecedented level, but the quality of what they are obsessed with is in a general decline.

Allan Bloom spoke at length (and quite eloquently) on this point in his book, *The Closing of the American Mind*. Commenting on our culture's obsession with music, he writes:

"It is available twenty-four hours a day, everywhere. There is the stereo in the home, in the car; there are concerts; there are music videos, with special channels exclusively devoted to them, on the air nonstop; there are the Walkmans so that no place—not public transportation, not the library—prevents students from communing with the Muse . . . ." [1]

This is profound and true. Music is all around us. But the disturbing irony is that so many can be obsessed with so little. One doesn't often hear Bach, Duke Ellington, or Aaron Copland blasting out of a boom box. Don't misunderstand me; I know it's beginning to sound as if I don't like rock or any kind of modern music, or that I think we should remain in the past. That's ridiculous—I grew up on rock and roll, and for most of my life that's what I have written and played. My lamentations are for what I think is a lack of real creativity and the absence of an atmosphere that would encourage and reward it. Incidentally, I am not saying this from the standpoint of an artist who believes he is above that criticism. I constantly struggle to escape the ordinary in my own work, and seldom succeed.

Over the years I have accumulated a rather large collection of recordings which covers the whole spectrum of musical styles. Lately I have found that there is rarely time to sit down and simply listen to music, but in one of those rare moments, I pulled a record off the shelf that I have not listened to for probably ten years. It was an early album by a little-known British group, Gentle Giant. I happened to notice the liner notes on the album which read:

"It is our goal to expand the frontiers of contemporary popular music at the risk of being very unpopular. We have recorded each composition with the one thought—that it should be unique, adventurous and fascinating. It has taken every shred of our combined musical and technical knowledge to achieve this."

I think they fulfilled their prophecy of their own obscurity, but what a credo! They stated most succinctly the exact attitude which I think is missing from so much of today's contemporary music. There is no virtue in intentionally seeking to be unpopular, nor does commercial success automatically mean that a piece of music was conceived for that purpose. The best possible scenario is one in which the highest creative endeavors are accessible to the broadest possible audience.

Bloom makes a point in his book with which I completely disagree. He maintains that the musical soil is rich, and that "There is no dearth of the new and the startling."[2] To the contrary, I find a tremendous dearth of the new, although I grant that some things I hear are indeed startling. I would have to take the position of Ecclesiastes—that there is nothing new under the sun. Virtually everything on the airwaves is so completely formularized that it sounds like it came off an assembly line. I don't really think that there is a total absence of creative musicians on the face of the earth. They surely exist in garages and basements, and might be heard on the most obscure private record labels, but obscurity is the key word here.

Ironically, there are some real virtuoso players out there, but the confines of the styles in which they are trapped can make them stupefyingly boring. Guitarists are particularly guilty of saturating the market with their machine-gun arpeggios and ever more flamboyant and postured chromatic explosions. How much more impressed are we supposed to get? The whole genre seems to be designed to draw attention to the player rather than the music.

Even the college radio stations with their "alternative music" suffer from a dreadful sameness. Most of the groups I hear on these stations seem to believe that providing an alternative consists of either imitating the bands of the sixties or being as cacophonous and obnoxious as possible.

There was indeed an explosion of creativity in the sixties and early seventies upon which we are still coasting. Many of the popular musicians of that decade literally defined how some instruments are played thirty years later. There is not a contemporary rock guitarist, for example, who does not owe a huge debt to Hendrix, Clapton, and others.

During that brief period, scores of new bands emerged, almost all of which had a distinctively individual and identifiable style. Musicians were doing many things that had never been done before. It was a very open and creative decade. We are now in an imitative period. I am amazed at the apparently unending number of heavy metal groups, for example, that are strapped with such rigid parameters in both their music and their appearance. Where are the individuals?

One of the things that frightens me most about saying things like this is that I sound just like our dads sounded when we were teenagers! Growing up in the sixties, most of us heard our parents expound on the unequaled greatness of Benny Goodman or Glenn Miller, and how this "modern" music sounded like noise, had no melody, and would not stand the test of time. The generational boundaries were clear then, but interestingly, they seem to be getting less distinct today.

I have seen many families with teenagers in which both

the parents and kids were listening to the same groups. In some cases, the kids were reaching farther back than the parents were. That rarely would have been the case in the sixties or even the seventies. I never would have bought a Count Basie or Frankie Carle album when I was sixteen (although I appreciate them now, and I'm starting to really dig Glenn Miller).

As a member of a band that reached its peak of popularity in the late seventies, I find it gratifying, but also peculiar, to be receiving a significant amount of fan mail from people 25 years younger than me. On the most recent Kansas tour, our audiences ranged from early teens to late middle age. Something has certainly changed.

The only theory I have for this is as follows: As modern music becomes more formularized, derivative, and shallow, listeners are crossing cultural and generational boundaries to find music of spiritual and creative substance. Witness the recent interest in various types of "ethnic" music. I find myself listening to it a lot because it seems so untainted and fresh—free from the corporate mold.

Christian music suffers from the same malady. Though we as Christians have a mandate to be skillful and creative, and Scripture affirms that we should sing unto the Lord a new song, we rarely hear anything truly new. The atmosphere of Christian radio is so limited as to be almost stifling. Not only is it as highly formatted as its secular counterpart, but in most cases, the artist must conform to some sort of spiritual criteria—someone's definition of what makes his or her music acceptable Christian music. It's a strange irony indeed that finds lyrics with the most profound truth coupled with the most unchallenging sort of muzak.

I have noted the church lowering its standard in other ways regarding art and music. The practice of singing to tape tracks rather than live musicians has invaded the church and become so prevalent as to become almost the norm. Though I understand why this is done, I can't get over the feeling that it is not an improvement, but a step down. I find it particularly repulsive in the context of a concert. I leave these events feeling like I've been to half a concert. I have no problem using things like sequencers and overdubbing for recording, but something precious is lost when a "live" performance is not alive. It deprives the musician of his place and the audience of the joy and spontaneity of human expression. I have even seen a "performance" on Christian television in which the music was on tape and the vocals were lip synced. Is this supposed to inspire?

Recently I have been listening to a recording of a composition by Ralph Vaughan Williams entitled "Ring Out Ye Crystal Spheres." I decided as I was listening that this piece embodies everything I find missing in contemporary popular music, Christian or secular. It is majestic, mysterious, uplifting, serenely beautiful, transcendent, moving, brimming over with power, inspiring, inspired, skillfully crafted, done to the glory of God, and totally fulfilling (I like it!). "But Kerry," you say, "I feel the same way about rap music." That's a difficult argument to counter. There truly is no accounting for taste, but it does not lessen my conviction that we are in the direst need of the above-mentioned qualities in our contemporary art, literature and music. They are sadly lacking. In fact, our culture has so re-defined art that the word has become meaningless. "Art" no longer represents the highest thoughts and aspirations of man. You can now walk down the main streets in America and find the pornographic theatres labeled as "Art Cinemas." "Art" no longer requires transcendent and inspired human skills to produce, and the word decadent falls hopelessly short of describing its moral status. It now includes the most repulsive sort of filth imaginable, all protected under the umbrella of free speech and artistic expression, and for society to set some standard as to what is acceptable, or to even describe a recording's contents with a label brings cries of "Fascist censorship! Don't impose your morality on me!" It would be interesting if the same standards that they want removed from their art were to be removed from the food they eat.

I can't help it, but something in me tells me that paint splattered on a canvas with a hose is not on a par with Rembrandt or Leonardo, rap and Thrash are not an improvement on Tchaikovsky or Debussy, and a crucifix in a jar of urine falls a little short of Michelangelo. If our art and our

music are the pulse of our culture, then civilization is sliding
down, and if we haven't hit bottom, how much lower can we go?

THE BIG LESSON

The Christian life is an unending series of lessons and instruction. Training in righteousness is no mean task. As I look back to the day of my conversion, I am first overwhelmed with thankfulness for God's mercy, and also amazed at how far I have come since that day.

Faith in Christ means the death of the old and the birth of the new, and birth is always followed by growth. Growth sometimes comes in spurts and at other times is agonizingly slow. I have experienced it both ways.

Every hour spent in the Scriptures brings about some new revelation or understanding. This never ceases to amaze me.

Ever since the first time I heard a good expository Bible teacher, I have been drawn to them like a moth to a flame. That can be a pitfall, for we are not to receive everything we hear without testing it and discerning whether or not it is valid, and that demands personal study.

I have, I suppose, a particular sensitivity for sound doctrine since I was delivered from a false one. Once a child has been burned, he's a little more wary of putting his hand in the fire.

In spite of my affinity for teachers, I never imagined I would be doing it myself. Somehow, most Christians resign themselves to be the sheep rather than the shepherds. Having always been a voracious reader, I soon acquired a rather large library of Christian writings after my conversion. I read C. S. Lewis, A. W. Tozer, D. Martyn Lloyd-Jones, and many other great

Christian writers. In addition, I devoured literally hundreds of taped lessons and sermons on cassette. What I didn't realize, was that God was holding me accountable for what I was learning.

The Lord has taught me so many things about myself and about Himself over the years that it's hard to say what has been the biggest lesson, but I would say that what He has shown me about the believer's relationship to the church has been one of the most significant in my life.

I had always imagined that my purpose on this planet was to make music and consisted of little else. I also assumed that it was my purpose in His church as well. I was only partly right. Most of what I have done in Christian music over the years was done apart from any direct involvement in a church body. I have always been faithful in attending church, but my level of involvement never consisted of anything more than mere membership. I viewed it as sort of a "home base;" a place that I went to get "charged up." I never consciously avoided being involved more deeply, I just didn't yet fully understand that the church is a body. It's easy to fall into the trap of being an "audience" in church. You will find nothing of this sort in the New Testament.

In the Scriptures, individual believers are compared to the parts and organs of a living body. There is no part of your body which does not in some way participate in the life of your body. There is no part of your body which is useless and without a purpose, however menial. They are all wonderfully designed to perform some task.

We are no different. To see ourselves only as recipients of the church is a grave mistake. True, we assemble together to learn and be nourished, but to what end? To serve! I sometimes hear Christians say, "I didn't get anything out of that service." My reply is, "What did you bring into it?"

Every Sunday there are thousands of sermons preached, Bible verses read, hymns sung, and lessons taught. Where is all this knowledge going?

Are you constantly getting closer to serving in the church, or just soaking it all up, walking out the door and going on with life as usual?

The day came when I knew I had to make the choice between being a hearer or a doer in my role in the church. It didn't actually happen in just a day, but rather over a period of months, and grew not out of one quick decision, but out of a gradually developing willingness to give in to God's will.

I had been doing a lot of speaking in churches and schools over the years, but I always was uncomfortable being asked to do it. Frankly, it bothered me that people felt that my "testimony" was any more important or valid than anyone else's. I knew that I never would have been asked if I had not held some sort of special position of popularity in the world, and that always ate at me. I felt that sometimes the church was parading Dave and me around like we were some sort of trophy. As new believers, we had both been on the 700 Club twice. I had no lack of enthusiasm for telling people about Christ, but I was just never at peace with the idea that we were asked to speak because of our notoriety.

Eventually I accepted this as part of the reality of my life, and resolved to use it to God's glory rather than complain about it. I do wish the church would give new believers more time to be established in the faith before making spectacles of them.

I also began to feel the desire to grow beyond just telling the story of how I came to believe, but I wasn't sure exactly what that meant. I knew that the Scriptures teach that every Christian receives one or more spiritual gifts with which we are to serve, but like many, I wasn't sure what mine were. I realized that just being a musician was not the fulfillment of this, since it is a natural gift and not a truly spiritual one.

I think many of us don't know what our gifts are because, in truth, we would not use them as we should if we did know. The surrender to His will, and our willingness to serve God in the capacity He desires will, I believe, remove any mystery as to what our gifts are.

After we moved to the farm, we began attending a nearby church, and I found after a short time in this small body that I was being asked to work in several ways in which I had no previous experience—serving on the church board and occasionally teaching the adult class. I was suddenly in a position of leadership, and as uncomfortable as it felt, I could not escape the conviction that it was what God would have me do. A soldier who sits on the sidelines in a war is not much use to anyone. The Lord has made it clear that much is expected from one to whom much is given, and I began to see a place emerging for me in God's Kingdom as a teacher. All that reading had caught up with me. It was exciting to discover a gift that I never knew I had, but also disturbing because I now knew that I would be held accountable to use it.

In a small church, it is much more likely that every believer will be asked to be a leader in some way rather than a follower, and one can only escape serving by making it clear that you are unwilling or unable to do so. It is also nearly impossible to maintain any sort of anonymity (which is an unacceptable desire anyway) in a small congregation.

I did not take this change in my spiritual life as any small thing. Teaching places one on an altogether different level of accountability, as does making decisions in guiding the church. I found that it drew me into prayer and Bible reading more than before, but most significant was the intensification of spiritual warfare. When you start being used of God, expect the enemy to step up his attacks, for now you are a greater threat to him. I was suddenly facing more temptations of every sort, and almost daily, I was fighting off a peculiar sort of spiritual lethargy. It was like a sweet seductive voice saying, "Back off . . . take it easy . . . it isn't worth it . . . these people don't care anyway . . . wouldn't you rather be using this time for yourself? You're not worthy to be doing this anyway." I'm sure any Christian with any sort of active ministry knows exactly what I'm talking about.

Even though a leadership position makes life harder, it also makes it more gratifying. I developed a love-hate relationship with teaching. It was so much easier to sit back and be taught than it was to pray and study and face down all the distractions that inevitably come. I both dreaded and looked forward to those occasions when I would teach or speak. And all this came about just as a result of doing it on an occasional basis.

I became very close to our new pastor, Rob Raynor. His first Sunday at this church was also my first Sunday, and I found him to be a kindred spirit in many ways. Being a pastor was new to him as well, as it was his first pastorate. He was largely responsible for motivating us to become more involved in the church on every level, and this subject was prominent in many of his sermons.

A time came in 1989 when some of the members of our church were led to start a new fellowship in our county. We wanted it to be a trans-denominational evangelical church which was biblically based, and which incorporated both some very traditional and modern approaches to worship. The previous pastor of our former church took over Rob's position, and we had our first meeting in the Raynors' living room. We decided to call it Grace Fellowship Church.

I've attended several churches in the last several years, but I never dreamed I would be pioneering one. I was only beginning to get used to the idea of being more actively involved when I found myself in a much more prominent position in this new church, with even more responsibilities. Rob was the preacher, and I was the only other teacher.

Actually, our roles weren't that easily defined. In a small new church, you'll often find yourself "wearing many hats" and fulfilling several different positions. On any given day I might find myself being a deacon, overseer, songleader, teacher, treasurer, or whatever else I was called upon to do.

In a matter of a few months this little church moved from a living room to a motel to a shopping center and finally to our own building.

One of the great things about teaching the adult class in our church is how much I learn. I never could have reached this level of discipline without having made the commitment to teach others. I have also enjoyed providing the music in our worship service, particularly the old hymns. They have stretched my musical skills much more than the contemporary praise songs (there I go again extolling the past!).

All this has been a very challenging endeavor, but one in which I have seen God work in remarkable ways, not only in the growth of the body but in my own life, which brings me to my main point.

Biblically speaking, a local church is not so much an organization as it is an organism composed of the lives of God's children in Christ. When we serve other members of the body of Christ, our service is rendered to the Lord. That is a picture that clearly emerges from the New Testament. I had never perceived my ministry as a Christian as being outside of the church, but I had never seriously considered the roles and positions for myself that the Scriptures lay out for us to fulfill in the local church. I had the proverbial cart in front of the horse.

I had never lacked zeal for my God, but I had always wanted to serve Him as I wanted to serve Him. I needed to learn to humble myself, even if it meant playing "Onward Christian Soldiers" on an out-of-tune piano in a little country church in Georgia. It does not mean that my more grandiose endeavors (books, recordings, tours, etc.) have been invalid or out of God's will, but I needed to learn to be obedient to God in the small things first. And remember that they are "small things" only in man's eyes, not God's. Being a vital part of the body of Christ is not an option for believers. Followers of Christ cannot cut themselves off from involvement with other believers any more than a limb or organ could be removed from the rest of the body and thrive.

Over and over I hear young Christians tell me that they have been called to a music ministry. I would not presume to question another Christian's calling, but it seems strange to me that God would call so many into contemporary Christian music and so few to minister to the immediate needs of His church.

Frankly, I think there is a choking glut of people with musical aspirations and too few who look first to see whether there might be some less glamorous way in which the Lord might want them to serve. If only we could remember (and I'm preaching to myself) that He would gratify the desires of our hearts if we would seek His Kingdom and His righteousness first.

I have not by any means forsaken my efforts in writing and recording music, and I still know that those things can be used of the Lord to His purposes, but I have come to learn that it is not the only way in which God wanted me to serve Him.

MUSIKS AND REUNIONS

I spent most of 1989 working on my first instrumental album, *One of Several Possible Musiks.* I must confess that I enjoyed making that album as much if not more than any I have worked on. Instrumental music was a new endeavor for me, and I found a musical freedom in it that was refreshing and fun. It seemed as if the boundaries of expression were much broader when not strapped with conforming to lyrics.

I realized, when I thought about it, that many of my favorite pieces of music were instrumental. I also realized that when I listened to them that I had never really separated them into a different category just because they were instrumental. In fact, in some ways they are more spiritual to me, as they express things that cannot be expressed in words. Words would only drag them down. It was almost intoxicating to have that freedom.

Since the album was to be released on a Christian label it occurred to me that some might ask the question: What makes this instrumental music "Christian?"

The answer is that it is an improper question. I don't believe that music, in and of itself, can necessarily be secular or spiritual. Does the fact that it was composed and performed by a Christian make the music Christian music? What if an unbeliever performs or sings a piece that was written to the glory of God? Can it still edify or inspire? What if a Christian writes a commercial—is it then a sanctified commercial? If I took an instrumental work that I composed before my conversion and re-titled it with some biblical theme, does it then become a piece of

Christian music? Conversely, one could conceivably take a sacred hymn, re-write the lyrics about some secular theme, and make it a popular song. Is the music itself then no longer spiritual?

I hope you can see my argument here—all good things come from God, and music is a good thing.

I will leave it at that. In my personal experience, many of my most worshipful moments which were inspired by music have come by the music of gifted men who did not know the God who gave them the gift.

I do, and He gets the glory. To me, that makes it Christian music.

Doing the *Musiks* album represented something of a shift in direction in my music career. As enjoyable as it was, I went back to work on vocal songs after I finished it. I was not really sure what I should do next, and it was during the early months of 1990 that I began to have frequent conversations with Phil Ehart, the drummer of Kansas.

Even though I had not been in the band for years, I had still been involved with the band on a business and corporate level. Dave and I were still a part of the "business." Phil and I still had discussions about royalty matters, expenses, etc.

As this line of communication opened up, we began to talk about what we were doing musically. At one point in time the "new" Kansas line-up which included Steve Morse on guitar was playing in Atlanta, and Phil invited me to come down and sit in on "Dust in the Wind."

Rob Raynor (my pastor-friend) and I drove to town with our families for the concert, and I made this brief re-appearance with the band. "Dust" is one of the few songs that we could have played with no rehearsal. It was great to see all the guys, and I have to admit that my heart fluttered a little when I took the stage again with Kansas.

I never suspected that it would lead to anything else. It was one thing to go see the guys for old times' sake, but I don't think they or I wanted it to be anything more than that at the time.

In the following months, things became very uncertain

for the "new" Kansas; they were out of a record deal, and Phil asked me if I would be interested in writing songs for the band to demo. By this time, A.D. was long gone, Steve Morse had left Kansas, and I was not sure what my next move should be. Steve Walsh came out to my studio and we worked on a couple of songs, and just got to know each other again. It felt good to hear him sing.

In spite of these things, I just couldn't picture myself in Kansas again, and I hadn't really been asked anyway. There had been so many changes in my life; changes in priorities, motives and methods, plus my commitments to my church and my family. Yet in the summer of 1990, Phil finally asked me if I would like to rejoin the band for a European tour. It would entail only a few weeks of our time, and would not wreak much havoc in anyone's life. I viewed it foremost as an opportunity to re-establish some strained friendships. Dave and I talked and prayed about it, and then came to a decision to do the reunion tour.

The first rehearsal was like being in "the Twilight Zone." It was as if someone had plucked me out of my life and placed me back in time. It took only a couple of days for the band to get in shape. Most of those songs are so deeply ingrained in me that it was like riding a bicycle; you never really forget how to do it.

The tour was perhaps the most enjoyable one I've ever been on. Having been put together by a German promoter, it was very organized and efficient. Most of all, the relationships between the guys in the band was better than they had ever been; everyone was going out of his way to make it fun and successful, and the band sounded great.

I had forgotten how powerful Kansas could be on stage. It was sobering and a little amazing to see once again the grip that music can hold on an audience. My heart ached for both the audience and the band members who did not know the God who had both created them and redeemed them. As I looked out over the cheering crowds, I reflected again on the long journey that had brought me to this moment, and I was overwhelmed with how good God has been to me. The whole experience re-awakened in me the desire to use every means I have to point people in the direction of the cross and the empty tomb.

I never imagined that I would have the opportunity to be a part of Kansas again, and I'm not sure where it will go from here, but this I do know: in the end it will not have mattered that I was a successful musician. It will not have mattered that I wrote a book or had a family or worked on a farm.

When all is said and done, and my life is over, all that will truly have mattered is that I made a choice in this life to believe in and serve the Lord Jesus Christ. Only the works I did for the furtherance of His Kingdom will have any lasting value. My hope is in His character and promises, and I know that this present life is not worthy of comparison to the life He is preparing for me.

I would like to leave you with the closing words of the book of Jude:

"To him who is able to keep you from falling and to present you before his glorious presence without fault and with great joy—to the only God our Savior be glory, majesty, power and authority, through Jesus Christ our Lord, before all ages, now and forevermore! Amen." (Jude 24-25)

NOTES

Chapter 4: The Quest Leads to the East

1. Hermann Hesse, *Steppenwolf* (New York: Bantam Books, 1963 [1927]), pp. 175, 176.
2. Hermann Hesse, *The Journey to the East* (New York: Bantam Books, 1961 [1932]), pp. 48, 49.
3. *Be Here Now* (San Cristobal, N.M.: Lama Foundation, 1971), p. 86.
4. D. T. Suzuki, *Zen Buddhism,* William Barrett, editor (Garden City, N.Y.: Doubleday, Anchor Books, 1956), pp. 112, 113.
5. Robert Sohl and Audrey Carr, editors, *The Gospel According to Zen* (New York: New American Library, Mentor Books, 1970), p. 11.
6. *Ibid.,* p. 23. This originally appeared in Alan Watts, *Beyond Theology* (New York: Pantheon Books, 1964), p. 229.
7. *Ibid.,* p. 49.
8. *Ibid.,* p. 72.
9. Watts, *Beyond Theology,* pp. 224, 225 (italics mine). See David K. Clark, *The Pantheism of Alan Watts* (Downers Grove, Ill.: InterVarsity Press, 1978) for a thoughtful critique of Watts' pantheistic world view.
10. Sri Chinmoy, *The Inner Promise* (New York: Simon and Schuster, Touchstone Books, 1971), p. 17.
11. *Ibid.,* p. 22.
12. *Ibid.,* pp. 38, 57.
13. *Ibid.,* pp. 77, 78.
14. *Ibid.,* p. 167.
15. Claudio Naranjo, *The One Quest* (New York: Viking Press, 1972), p. 202.
16. *Ibid.,* p. 136.
17. J. Krishnamurti, *Think on These Things* (New York: Harper & Row, Perennial Library, 1964), p. 57.
18. *Ibid.,* p. 81.
19. *Ibid.,* p. 93.
20. *The Spiritual Teaching of Ramana Maharshi* (Berkeley, Calif.: Shambala, Clear Light Series, 1972), p. 10.
21. *Ibid.,* p. 71.
22. *Tao, A Rendering into English Verse of the Tao Teh Ching of Lao Tsze,* trans. by Charles A. Mackintosh (Wheaton, Ill.: Theosophical Publishing House, 1926), pp. 43, 44, 46, 68.

23. *The I Ching or Book of Changes,* the Richard Wilhelm translation rendered into English by Cary F. Baynes, Bollingen Series XIX (Princeton, N.J.: Princeton University Press for Bollingen Foundation, Inc., 1950); and Da Liu, *I Ching Coin Prediction* (New York: Harper & Row, 1975).

24. Thaddeus Golas, *The Lazy Man's Guide to Enlightenment* (Palo Alto, Calif.: Seed Center, 1971), p. 13.

25. William Irwin Thompson, *Passages About Earth* (New York: Harper & Row, Perennial Library, 1973), p. 97.

26. *Ibid.,* p. 188.

27. *Ibid.,* p. 153. *Passages About Earth* builds upon many of the themes developed in Thompson's earlier book, *At the Edge of History* (New York: Harper & Row, 1971).

28. Paramahansa Yogananda, *Autobiography of a Yogi* (Los Angeles: Self-Realization Fellowship, 1972 [1946]), p. 9.

29. *Ibid.,* pp. 216, 217.

30. *Ibid.,* pp. 395, 396; also pp. 475-497.

31. *Ibid.,* p. 169.

32. *Ibid.,* p. 347.

33. *Ibid.,* p. 403.

34. Nikos Kazantzakis, *Report to Greco,* trans. by P. A. Bien (New York: Bantam Books, 1966 [1961]), p. 9.

35. *Ibid.,* p. 141.

36. *Ibid.,* pp. 213, 214.

37. *Ibid.,* p. 144.

38. *Ibid.,* p. 277.

39. Jane Roberts, *Seth Speaks* (New York: Bantam Books, 1972), p. 416.

40. *Ibid.,* p. 387.

41. *Ibid.,* p. 384.

42. *Ibid.,* pp. xv-xvi.

43. *Ibid.,* front cover.

44. Richard Bach, *Jonathan Livingston Seagull* (New York: Avon Books, 1970), p. 80.

45. *Ibid.,* pp. 120, 124.

Chapter 5: Musical Influences

1. Back cover notes for the Columbia album, *Thomas Schippers Conducts Barber:* New York Philharmonic.

2. As translated by Peggie Cochrane in the notes for the RCA album, *Mahler—Symphony of a Thousand* (Symphonica of London, Wyn Morris, Conductor).

3. ©by Maclen Music, Inc. All rights reserved.

4. From the record sleeve of *In Search of the Lost Chord* by The Moody Blues, Decca Record Company Limited, 1968.

5. Geoffrey Parrinder, *A Dictionary of Non-Christian Religions* (Philadelphia: Westminster Press, 1971), p. 208.

Chapter 7: The Music of Kansas

1. ©1973 Don Kirshner Music, Inc. (BMI). Used by permission. All rights reserved.

2. ©1974 Don Kirshner Music, Inc. (BMI). Used by permission. All rights reserved.

3. *Ibid.*

4. ©1975 Don Kirshner Music, Inc. (BMI). Used by permission. All rights reserved.

5. *Ibid.*

6. André Pieyre de Mandiargues, *Arcimboldo the Marvelous* (New York: Harry N. Abrams, Inc., 1978), p. 72.

7. ©1975 Don Kirshner Music, Inc. (BMI). Used by permission. All rights reserved.

8. *Ibid.*

9. *Ibid.*

10. *Ibid.*

11. ©1976 Don Kirshner Music, Inc. (BMI). Used by permission. All rights reserved.

12. *Ibid.*

13. *Ibid.*

14. *Ibid.*

15. *Ibid.*

16. ©1977 Don Kirshner Music, Inc. (BMI). Used by permission. All rights reserved.

17. *Ibid.*

18. Francis A. Schaeffer, *How Should We Then Live?* (Old Tappan, N.J.: Fleming H. Revell Company, 1976), and *A Christian Manifesto* (Westchester, Ill.: Crossway Books, 1981).

19. ©1977 Don Kirshner Music, Inc. (BMI). Used by permission. All rights reserved.

20. *Ibid.*

21. ©1979 Don Kirshner Music/Blackwood Music Publishing (BMI). Used by permission. All rights reserved.

Chapter 8: Urantia

1. *Bhagavad Gita,* trans. by Sir Edwin Arnold (New York: Heritage Press, 1965), chap. xi.

2. "Urantia," a brochure inserted in *The Urantia Book.*

3. Dean Halverson, "Urantia . . . the Brotherhood, the Book," *SCP Newsletter,* August 1981, pp. 1, 3.

4. *Ibid.,* p. 3.

5. Ruth Barton, "Basic Concepts of *The Urantia Book*" (Urantia Brotherhood, 1977), quoted in Dean Halverson, "Urantia . . . the Brotherhood, the Book," p. 5.

6. *The Urantia Book* (Chicago: Urantia Foundation, 1955), p. 129.

7. *Ibid.,* p. 17.

8. ©1979 Don Kirshner Music/Blackwood Music Publishing (BMI). Used by permission. All rights reserved.

Chapter 9: The Door Opens At Last

1. *The Urantia Book*, p. 2003.
2. *Ibid.*, p. 1670.
3. Colossians 2:8-10. See also Dean Halverson, "Urantia . . . the Brotherhood, the Book," p. 5.
4. *Urantia*, p. 1670.
5. Genesis 3:5.
6. John 7:17.
7. Ephesians 6:11, 12.
8. 2 Corinthians 11:13-15.

Chapter 10: A New Beginning

1. John 1:1-4, 14; Colossians 1:16, 17; Hebrews 1:2, 3.
2. 2 Corinthians 5:17.
3. Galatians 5:22, 23.
4. John 3:3.
5. Matthew 13:57.

Chapter 11: Three More Albums

1. Revelation 22:13.
2. John 14:6; Acts 4:12; 1 Timothy 2:5.
3. ©1980 Don Kirshner Music/Blackwood Music Publishing (BMI). Used by permission. All rights reserved.
4. John 8:31, 32.
5. John 16:11; Ephesians 2:2.
6. ©1980 Don Kirshner Music/Blackwood Music Publishing (BMI). Used by permission. All rights reserved.
7. *Ibid.*
8. Mark 10:45.
9. Matthew 24:24.
10. Matthew 24:27.
11. ©1980 Don Kirshner Music/Blackwood Music Publishing (BMI). Used by permission. All rights reserved.
12. *Ibid.*
13. Matthew 6:10.
14. ©1982 Don Kirshner Music/Blackwood Music Publishing (BMI). Used by permission. All rights reserved.
15. John 11:50.
16. ©1982 Don Kirshner Music/Blackwood Music Publishing (BMI). Used by permission. All rights reserved.
17. 1 John 2:16, 17.
18. ©1982 Don Kirshner Music/Blackwood Music Publishing (BMI). Used by permission. All rights reserved.
19. 2 Corinthians 5:7; also see 2 Corinthians 4:18.
20. ©1982 Don Kirshner Music/Blackwood Music Publishing (BMI). Used by permission. All rights reserved.
21. ©1982 Don Kirshner Music/Blackwood Music Publishing, Full Grown Music and Mastodon Music (BMI). Used by permission. All rights reserved.

22. Revelation 22:16; also see 2 Peter 1:19.
23. ©1982 Don Kirshner Music/Blackwood Music Publishing, Full Grown Music and Mastodon Music (BMI). Used by permission. All rights reserved.
24. ©1982 Don Kirshner Music/Blackwood Music Publishing (BMI). Used by permission. All rights reserved.
25. Romans 5:6-8.

Chapter 12: The Art of Rock

1. Exodus 35:31.
2. William A. Dyrness, "Creativity and the Christian Artist," *Radix Magazine,* March/April 1982, p. 20.
3. Steve Lawhead, *Rock Reconsidered* (Downers Grove, Ill.: InterVarsity Press, 1981), p. 59.
4. *Ibid.,* p. 61.
5. *Ibid.,* p. 67.
6. Francis A. Schaeffer, *Art and the Bible* (Downers Grove, Ill.: InterVarsity Press, 1973), pp. 41-48.
7. *Ibid.,* p. 42.
8. Lawhead, *Rock,* p. 129.
9. Schaeffer, p. 47.
10. See 1 Corinthians 5:9-13.
11. 1 Corinthians 9:22.

Chapter 15: Soapbox

1. Allan Bloom, *The Closing of the American Mind* (New York: Simon and Schuster, 1987) p. 68.
2. *Ibid.,* p. 69.

KANSAS PRODUCED BY WALLY GOLD, KIRSHNER/CBS
RELEASED: 1974 BY KANSAS. EPC80174

TIMELINE PRODUCED BY KERRY LIVGREN, CBS ASSOCIATED
RELEASED: 1984 BY KERRY LIVGREN/AD. BFZ39368

SONG FOR AMERICA PRODUCED BY MALLY GOLD/JEFF GLIXMAN
KIRSHNER/CBS. RELEASED: 1975 BY KANSAS

THE BEST OF KANSAS PRODUCED BY VA`RIOUS PRODUCERS. CBS
ASSOCIATED. RELEASED: 1984 BY KANSAS

MASQUE PRODUCED BY JEFF GLIXMAN, KIRSHNER/CBS
RELEASED: 1975 BY KANSAS. PZ33806

ART OF THE STATE PRODUCED BY KERRY LIVGREN, KERYGMA/SPARROW
RELEASED: 1985 BY AD KRC/D5401

LEFTOVERTURE PRODUCED BY JEFF GLIXMAN
KIRSHNER/CBS. RELEASED: 1976 BY KANSAS

RECONSTRUCTIONS PRODUCED BY KERRY LIVGREN, KERYGMA/SPARROW
RELEASED: 1986 BY AD

POINT OF KNOW RETURN PRODUCED BY JEFF GLIXMAN
KIRSHNER/CBS RELEASED: 1977 BY KANSAS. JZ34929

PRIME MOVER PRODUCED BY KERRY LIVGREN, SPARROW
RELEASED: 1988 BY KERRY LIVGREN/AD. SPC/D1181

TWO FOR THE SHOW PRODUCED BY KANSAS KIRSHNER/CBS
RELEASED: 1978 BY KANSAS. PZ235660

ONE OF SEVERAL POSSIBLE MUSIKS PRODUCED BY KERRY LIVGREN,
SPARROW. RELEASED: 1989 BY KERRY LIVGREN SPC/D1200

MONOLITH PRODUCED BY KANSAS, KIRSHNER/CBS
RELEASED: 1979 BY KANSAS FZ36008

SEEDS OF CHANGE PRODUCED BY KERRY LIVGREN/BRAD AARON
KIRSHNER/CBS. RELEASED: 1980 BY KERRY LIVGREN. NJ236567

AUDIOVISIONS PRODUCED BY KANSAS, KIRSHNER/CBS
RELEASED: 1980 BY KANSAS. FZ36588

VINYL CONFESSIONS PRODUCED BY KANSAS/KEN SCOTT
CBS ASSOCIATED. RELEASED: 1982 BY KANSAS. HZ48002

DRASTIC MEASURES PRODUCED BY KANSAS/NEIL KERNAN
CBS ASSOCIATED. RELEASED: 1983 OZ38733